The Christmas Stories

Ted Field

authorHOUSE®

AuthorHouse™
1663 Liberty Drive
Bloomington, IN 47403
www.authorhouse.com
Phone: 1 (800) 839-8640

Published by AuthorHouse   12/05/2016

ISBN: 978-1-5246-5359-0 (sc)
ISBN: 978-1-5246-5357-6 (hc)
ISBN: 978-1-5246-5358-3 (e)

Library of Congress Control Number: 2016920157

Print information available on the last page.

This book is printed on acid-free paper.

The Stories

To the congregation
of St Stephen Lutheran Church,
White Bear Lake, MN

Introduction

Christmas is our most beloved holiday. No other holiday is so richly decorated, seasoned by gladness, or trumpeted with music. We seem to behave better at Christmas. And even secularists celebrate the holiday as the highest altar of peace, love, and joy.

What's more, Christmas is a season, not a single day, which means its message of good cheer shines in the corners of our lives for weeks. Including Advent and the fact that the Twelve Days of Christmas don't begin until the 25th, Christians celebrate for a month. It can wear us out. We may admit after all the presents are opened and the floor under the tree is carpeted with dry needles that the season is too long. The kids need to get back in school and we need a rest.

Christmas is too big to be celebrated in one particular way. It is a kaleidoscope of rituals: tilt your head and you see something else to do. In no particular order, it is the exchange of gifts, the way kids revere Santa Claus, parties with friends, the gathering of families, hanging lights and decorating trees, baking cookies and exchanging cards, caroling and re-telling the same stories year after year, television specials, *It's A Wonderful Life*, and Tiny Tim proclaiming *God bless us, one and all*. There's much to do. Choose from the list how you want to celebrate your Christmas.

I wrote the pieces in *The Christmas Stories* over several years as an intentional attempt to highlight as many of the Christmas rituals as I could—and discover a deeper meaning in them. Beginning in 1999 I was asked each year to write and read aloud a story for the annual advent service led by the senior choir of St Stephen Lutheran Church in White Bear Lake, Minnesota. I ended up writing twenty stories and all are assembled here.

Because my assignment each year came without any conditions or restrictions regarding subject, I was free to explore Christmas's wide themes and horizons, using mostly personal experiences. Regretfully, on occasion I drifted outside the limits of decorum, like the year I told a story about getting drunk at a Christmas party. But, mostly, the task has given me purpose to reach back and relive many pleasant Christmas memories of my own.

Not all the stories are factual. Truthful maybe, but not factual. There is a difference. Truth encompasses things about our human condition we don't question even when they are presented to us in fiction. As examples, we know that we go home every Christmas, even if it's just a journey of the heart; that waiting for Christmas Day to arrive one slow day at a time is agonizing for children; that we are all one family at Christmas; and that the peace of Christmas can be more meaningful to those whose job is to preserve it. These are the truths about the holiday that can be told through works of fiction. Like Bible lessons, stories about our holiday traditions can be parables, too.

I wrote the stories to entertain but also to create touchstones for my personal journey in Christian faith. Many of my holiday traditions—like yours—are of the *Happy Holidays* variety bringing great joy but with seemingly few connections to Christ's birth. But I believe they all have connections. In these stories I have tried to show how each tradition is threaded with the real meaning of the holiday, which is a celebration of the original Christmas Story (yes, even getting drunk at a Christmas party has a faith message). That's why I chose for this collection the simple title *Christmas Stories*. The love and humanity of the first Christmas are present in our modern holiday traditions. A holy night in Bethlehem, an overcrowded inn, a guiding star, the manger, and the shepherds and wise men who travelled there have meaning in all the ways celebrate today.

We celebrate Christmas with friends and families, but it is also a time for personal reflection. All of us have our own special memories of the season, and one of my purposes in assembling this collection is to help you remember why the season is important to you. You have your own stories to keep. Write them down. Pass them on. They will always be special—and timeless—just like the original Christmas Story.

Ted Field
St Stephen Lutheran Church
Christmas, 2017

Good Receivers

1999

T**is the season of giving**. And receiving. At Christmas we call it giving—rather than receiving—gifts, even though the transaction requires both. One doesn't happen without the other. It's like a game of catch, needing two people, one to throw and one to catch. But we don't call it a game of throw. By its name, we take the throwing for granted and place the greater burden on catching the ball. The success is in the receiving.

Giving gifts may be an important ritual of Christmas but I submit that more responsibility for a good Christmas gift exchange should fall on the receiver. Good receiving can be hard, particularly when it's a gift that challenges the limits of your appreciation, like a tie resembling all the others hanging in your closet. It's like a game of catch where not every throw hits you in the hands.

My brother was an honest, if not diplomatic, gift receiver. A distant aunt once sent him a dress shirt that he didn't care for. It was a nice shirt, but just too highfalutin for his Salvation Army tastes. When he told me he was impartial to the shirt, I remarked how much I liked it and he tossed it to me in a quick exchange of ownership.

"Here," he said. "It's yours."

Fulfilling his responsibility to send a thank-you note, he took the honest path and confessed to the aunt what he had done, pointing out the double benefit of his act. He wrote that Ted loved the shirt while he was touched by the thought behind the gift, something *he* was able to keep. Two gifts for the price of one. A gift that keeps on giving.

But in truth he got the better end of the deal. He received the genuine emotion from someone who cared for him, while all I got was the symbol of that emotion. The shirt wore out one day, but the emotion never did.

Sometimes it's hard to find the emotional intent. At those times it's a challenge to remember that the thought behind the gift should be honored, rather than the gift itself.

One of my favorite stories about Christmas receiving comes from a novel called *Sometimes A Great Notion*. It's not a book about Christmas, but rather the story of a bunch of roughneck Oregon loggers, the Stamper family, led by older brother Hank.

The Stampers were brawlers, attracted to fisticuffs and bloody noses. The exception was Hank's cousin Joe Ben, whose charitable and optimistic nature contrasted sharply with the combative approach to life of the rest of the family, and Hank in particular. Joe Ben was kind and generous and believed everyone else was too. He had grown up viewing the world as a simple place filled with people of good intentions. He smiled at everything. To Hank and the others, Joe Ben had a tinker toy mind. During the day, as he worked amidst the roar of chain saws and crashing timber, he sang to the music playing on a transistor radio that hung from his neck.

The Stampers were not rich, so there were never piles of presents under the Christmas tree. As loggers eking out a living in the woods, they didn't have any trouble getting a tree, but decorating it was not always easy. So, every year when they were young, the Stamper boys got presents that were limited to whatever their stockings could hold: candy and yo-yo's and marbles and such. But on Christmas morning every year Joe Ben cheerfully sifted through the spare contents of his stocking and expressed his gratitude that Santa Claus had once again included him in his rounds. He always saw good fortune in his gifts before anyone else did.

Joe Ben's unbridled glee irritated his cousins to the point that one year Hank decided to pull a nasty trick on him. As boys, they lived in the same house, and late on Christmas Eve, after Santa had come and gone, Hank snuck downstairs, careful not to awaken the others. He took Joe Ben's stocking down from the mantle and emptied it and filled it with horse manure. Giggling to himself, he re-hung the stocking and slipped back into bed.

In the morning the boys dashed to the fireplace. Joe Ben grabbed his stocking and peered inside. His eyes grew wide as saucers. Then he suddenly dropped the stocking and ran to the front door. Hank, holding back a chuckle, asked, "Joe, where you goin'? What did ol' Santa bring you?"

Joe Ben reached for a piece of rope hanging from a hook by the door and answered, "Brought me a bran' new pony, but he got away. I'll catch him if I hurry." And then he ran out the door.

If someone had showed Joe Ben there was no pony, only a bad joke, he would have thanked the giver of the fertilizer and started a vegetable garden. He may have been holding the gift of a bad intention, but it was still a gift—with an intention of some kind—and he couldn't help but look beyond it in search of some good emotion that accompanies any gift. He was thankful, a good receiver.

This year, let's be like Joe Ben and dream of ponies, but be thankful of fertilizer. Let's not overlook the emotions behind the gifts. As we all know, the best gifts, large or small, come from the heart. Let's remember what the gifts are: the symbols of something that connects us every year at this time. Let's be good Christmas receivers.

It's been said that the wise men started the tradition of Christmas giving with the gifts they brought to the manger. They placed frankincense and myrrh at Mary's feet and stepped back to admire the Christ child. But, really, who was giving and who was receiving that night? And for the past two thousand years, every Christmas we celebrate again receiving God's greatest gift. We try to be good receivers. We're given the same gift every Christmas and unwrap it with the same wonder, joy and thanks. Year after year it goes on. It's been like a good game of catch.

Waiting for Christmas

2000

My grandmother had an expression that comes to mind this time of year. Anytime she thought I was moving too slowly and ordered me to speed up, I would always reply, "I'm coming", and then she got in the last word. "So is Christmas. You're as slow as Christmas."

These are words every child understands and knows to be true. Nothing is as slow as Christmas. Nothing *approaches* you slower than Christmas. The weeks leading up to Santa's arrival move imperceptibly with the speed of a glacier. For kids, the wait is agonizing, while grown-ups embrace the wait and even give it a name—*advent*—and celebrate it as a special event of its own. There is as much joy in knowing something wonderful is coming and having to wait for it as there is in actually experiencing it. We prefer a slow and sweet approach to Christmas but try explaining this to a child and he'll look at you like you have mistletoe sticking out your nose. Wait for Christmas? Are you crazy?

Christmas can't come too fast for a kid.

My father told me a story from his youth about a year he had to wait longer than usual for Christmas to arrive. It was the year he turned ten.

As usual, my father—Bill—went to bed on Christmas Eve with such anticipation of the next morning that sleep would not come, so he rose from his bed and sat at his bedroom window to look out over a neighborhood of snow-covered rooftops. This was Michigan's Upper Peninsula, where it always snowed. To say *White Christmas* in the U.P. is to repeat yourself.

His bedroom view took in countless chimneys, something his own house lacked. He was still young enough to believe that Santa Claus was on his way with a toy list that included Bill's name. He was sure he passed the "naughty or nice" test. After all, if every broken window or eruption of profanity sentenced a boy to the "naughty" column, Santa might as well cancel his trip and stay at the Pole on Christmas.

Bill's father had no trouble convincing Bill that the lack of a fireplace in their home wouldn't stop Santa from entering the house. He would use some other portal, like, say, the front door. *Of course. It had to be.* Surely, Santa's talents included the house-entering skills of a burglar.

Bill lay down and finally fell asleep. When he awoke, his room was still dark. Outside, the dim light of dawn was on the horizon, but there was nothing dim about his eagerness to get downstairs and see what Santa had left him.

He had been advised not to get up so early, so he quietly tip-toed down the stairs to the living room, which was also dark as a cave. He chose not to turn on a lamp and instead relied on his keen memory of the room's space and furniture layout to advance to the corner where he knew the Christmas tree stood over a bounteous assemblage of presents. Dropping to his knees, he felt underneath. The moment he had been dreaming about for months had finally arrived.

But there was nothing there.

His hand struck the bare hardwood floor and nothing else.

What?

He extended his reach further to the other side of the tree. Still nothing. A panic seize him. He crawled to an end table and reached for the lamp. Convinced that Santa had left gifts somewhere else in the room, he turned it on to look. *Still nothing.* There wasn't a toy or a ribbon or a bow in the entire room. Even the stockings were flat-empty.

There are many things that can devastate a ten-year old, but nothing can utterly crush him as much as the realization that the biggest day of the year has passed him by. The wishes and expectations, the anxious weeks of waiting, the promise of Christmas—everything leading up to this single moment of reward had failed Bill and left him with an emptiness that made him ill. As unimaginable as it seemed, inexplicably, Santa had missed him and would not be back for another year.

All this struck him in a matter of seconds.

Bill dropped to his knees and began to cry, so loud that he awoke his father, who put on a bathrobe and came downstairs muttering to himself. When he saw Bill, he didn't have to ask why he was up at the early hour— he knew why—and rather than scold him he crossed to room to give his son a hug. Then, he assessed the situation.

With Bill at his side, he walked around the house and into front hallway, where he found an important clue to the calamity: the front door was locked. Grasping for hope of any kind, Bill wiped his tears and watched his father turn the deadbolt and swing the door open. Together, they peered out through the storm door.

It had snowed the night before. Again.

In the blue, pre-dawn light, Bill could see that the front step and yard and sidewalk lay under a blanket of fresh, unbroken snow. There wasn't even the trace of a footprint. Bill looked up at his father. He wanted to believe so much that *this* was it, the cause of the problem. In moments of crisis, kids place their highest trust in their parents.

"Son," his father said, "let's go back to bed. I think Santa will try us again if we go back to bed. What do you say?"

What *could* he say? He had no other choice. Giving Santa a second chance was unheard of, but what did he have to lose?

Bill nodded and mumbled a few words of approval. His father turned off the lamp and they went up the stairs. His father tucked him in and assured him everything would be fine. Somehow, Bill was able to rid the crisis from his mind and fall asleep again.

Three hours later he awoke to a room bright with morning sunshine. He rushed downstairs and peered into the living room. Under the tree lay a sled and a football and other presents. The stockings on the fireplace bulged and sagged with great promise. Santa had come! He had really come! Shortly, the rest of his family joined in his celebration of Christmas's arrival. His father watched Bill move happily from toy to toy and then commented that Santa just needed a little more time to come this year.

The pre-dawn events of that morning came back to Bill, and after a moment of private reflection he set his new toys down and moved to the front door. He grasped the doorknob and pulled, and when the unlocked door swung open easily, he nodded with approval. The simple opening of the door was enough for him to accept what had happened, but when his gaze wandered out beyond the doorway and across the front yard, he found the clincher.

There was a carpet of clean, white snow extending smooth and unmarked out to the street, covering everything up to the door, except for the newspaper rolled up and laying out by the curb, and....something else. The snow on the front steps was trampled by boot prints, which also made a trail down the steps and across the yard and around the edge of the house to some unknown source—and destination—behind the garage. The line of prints was straight and purposeful. In a landscape of new-fallen snow, the prints were out of place and beyond explanation.

Bill couldn't take his eyes off the tracks. He stood there at the door until finally his father came to his side. Bill peered up at him for some confirmation of what he was seeing.

"Yeah," his father said. "Santa just needed a way to get into the house. Sometimes he needs a little help." Bill nodded.

My father told me this story when I was the same age he had been when it happened. In my immediate reaction I was spellbound by a story proving the existence of Santa. Great news! And, besides the importance of keeping the fireplace clean, I thought the lesson was that great disappointment is always lurking and can settle on us unexpectedly. But I missed the real message. The story really is about the absolute certainty that Christmas will come. The story tells me to have faith. Don't worry about its arrival. Kids will fret, and they'll value Christmas by the presents under the tree while adults will value it for something more, but either way, there is great joy when it comes. We sense it long before it happens. And when we are certain of its arrival, we revel in the anticipation. Waiting brings the same joy. We don't agonize over the wait. We welcome it, because Christmas always comes.

The Christmas Party

2001

Thirty years ago this week I joined the Army and prepared to spend Christmas away from home for the first time in my life.

I left home with light luggage. Besides a toothbrush, a change of underwear, and a paperback novel, I carried only the simple advice of a friend who had recently been discharged from the military. He told me, "Ted, whatever you do, don't ever, *ever* volunteer for anything in the Army. Nothing good comes from volunteering. It can only get you into trouble." The advice lacked any trace of holiday cheer but I still regarded it as an early Christmas gift.

I remember leaving home. It was a cold night in early December and my father drove me to the bus station in Alexandria. As the Trailways bus to Richmond pulled in to load, we stood on the sidewalk and said our goodbyes.

Dad recognized the moment as a parental milestone and that we were observing a rite of passage.

"I never imagined it would be like this," he said. "I pictured you going off to a job and getting your own place, starting a career, maybe close to home. But look at you." He was commenting on the sparseness of the belongings I carried, literally the clothes on my back and a rucksack over my shoulder. The Army wants you to leave home that way. They're waiting for you at the other end with everything you'll need. In that way, Army is a lot like camp.

The next day I was in the barracks in Kentucky to start boot camp.

My adjustment to basic training didn't go well. During my first week, for some unknown reason, I couldn't sleep. Despite long, rigorous days I lay at night wide-eyed in my top bunk staring at the high dark ceiling and struggling with my awakened state, listening to the barracks creak and moan against the wind outside and other recruits like me stirring restlessly in their bunks or moving about. Maybe the new surroundings were the cause of my insomnia. Or maybe it was my uncertain future in an overseas war. I never figured it out.

Whatever the cause, I knew I couldn't go on like this. Eventually, I would *have* to sleep. I felt that I needed just one good night's snooze to recharge. Without it, my condition would undo me in some unexpected and calamitous way, like a fumble on the hand grenade range. Or maybe my general health would deteriorate to the point I couldn't think or function. Restricted to only the barracks and mess hall, I couldn't get to the PX to buy a chemical aid for this sort of problem, so there seemed to be no cure other than to wait for my mind and body to reach their absolute limits of endurance and succumb to exhaustion on the verge of unconsciousness.

Meanwhile, I rose each morning to revile and struggled through the routines of boot camp orientation. Christmas liberty was two weeks way. My problem needed a solution sooner than that.

Then, on the sixth day, a fix appeared on the horizon. Our drill sergeant gave us some good news. That evening, all of us in the barracks would be granted a short liberty, two hours at the enlisted men's club at the end of the street, nothing ritzy, just a place where we could play cards, listen to music on a juke box, play ping-pong, or shoot pool. Or, for refreshment, drink some beer.

Beer.

Perhaps the tonic for my problem.

Applied in a proper dosage for medicinal purposes, liquid barley could create the proper state of drowsiness I badly needed. I was certainly familiar with its effects but had never used it as an intentional sleeping aid. Experience had taught me it would work.

So, after chow, I rushed down to the club to begin my treatment.

The club was a spartan place. Several small tables and folding chairs were scattered around a dimly lit room. The floor was linoleum and the walls were bare sheetrock. There was a pinball machine and a pool table. No Christmas decorations anywhere. The only seasonal tune on the jukebox was the Beach Boys singing *Santa's Souped-Up Sleigh*. Beer could be purchased from a vending machine for twenty-five cents a can. I found an empty chair and dug through my pockets for change and went to work.

I accepted my task with focused intent. Eyeing me curiously, my table mates questioned my well being. But an hour and a buck-and-a-half later there was a numbness in my lips and an echo in my ears. The room was spinning and the Beach Boys were sounding like Alvin and the Chipmunks.

My heavy eyelids and slurred speech told me that my treatment was complete. I rose to my feet and bid my friends goodnight. I walked toward the doorway, accidentally bumping my shoulder on the jamb, and fell outside. With proper bearing I staggered up the street toward the barracks where a warm bunk and a peaceful night's rest awaited me.

It was still early in the evening. Other recruits were walking up and down the street enjoying the cool December air. But most were heading away from the barracks—not toward it—to start their short liberty.

It was warm inside the barracks and I began taking off my coat even before I reached my bunk. But something was going on nearby, something peculiar. Even in my semi-alert state I could sense it. Not everyone had left the barracks for the evening and in the aisle between rows of bunks several recruits were gathered in conversion with the drill sergeant, who could strike fear in me during the day, but tonight, after hours, he posed no threat. Or so I thought.

By the worried expressions on the faces of the recruits encircling him, I guessed that the discussion was not a light one, and out of curiosity I slid closer and leaned in to listen. It would be my fatal mistake.

The sergeant was seeking four volunteers to attend a Christmas party. And he wasn't getting any takers. He kept repeating his offer, growing angrier each time, his voice rising and jaw clenched. Even inside, he wore his Smoky-the-Bear hat, its broad brim casting a frightful shadow over his face as he spoke.

Christmas party? We're invited to a Christmas party?

The advice of my friend back home, *never volunteer, it only gets you into trouble*, blared like a horn in my mind's fog. One of the recruits next to the sergeant challenged him to be honest and admit *there was no party*, just a work detail that needed four unsuspecting fools at this late hour. The other recruits nodded. I was too tired to move my head. But I knew he was right.

Disappointed at the reaction of wariness to his offer, the sergeant took matters into his own hands—"*Okay, boys, if that's the way you want it…*"—and decided to pick the lucky quartet himself. He revolved slowly, jabbing a straightened finger into the chests of some of the men around him, and counting—*one, two, three*—until he was facing me. I felt his finger lance me and heard him bellow "Four! The four of you! Outside now! In the car! On the double!"

17

I was stunned. I looked at him in disbelief. This can't be! Not tonight. I can't go on a work detail tonight. Not in my present condition, not when I have an appointment with my pillow and precious sleep was about to descend on me. But his icy stare was all the confirmation I needed that the dream had become a nightmare. Sadly, I put on my coat and went outside with the other three appointees and took a seat in the back of the sergeant's car.

As the sergeant drove away in the dark, the four of us were silent to our misfortune. Fighting off the urge to close my eyes and sleep, I imagined the job waiting ahead: mopping a floor or sweeping out an office or washing dishes in a mess hall. Miserable jobs didn't have to end at five o'clock. Oh well, I thought, if we could get the job done quickly, there would still be several hours left for my night of peaceful slumber.

The sergeant parked in front of an officer's club. By the number of cars outside, it was clear something was going on inside. K.P., I told myself. We'll be working the kitchen tonight. Maybe an hour, two if we're unlucky. The sergeant led us through the front door into a big room decorated for the holidays with wreaths and colored lights hanging everywhere, crowds of people, tables and chairs, music and the smell of food. We were met by an attractive woman in a party dress.

"Good evening, boys," she said pleasantly. "Thank you, sergeant. You can pick them up in two hours."

I was right. The Budweiser hadn't dulled my skill for time management.

She asked that we follow her and as we walked through the crowded, noisy room she engaged us in pleasant talk about our hometowns. They were mostly one-sided conversations. I was curious that she was leading us away from the kitchen and into the midst of party revelry, to a row of sofas and padded arm chairs arranged at the edge of a dance floor lit by overhead floodlights. There, she motioned for us to sit.

Then, all preconceptions of the evening vanished in a moment of clarifying sobriety.

Other women descended upon us angel-like with greetings and offerings of food. We were served glasses of fruit punch. We were given our own cookie tray. The lights in the room darkened, except for those over the dance floor, and from behind a curtain came children who performed the Christmas Story.

Later, Santa appeared and someone recited *The Night Before Christmas*. Our hostess took a seat at the piano and led the crowd in singing carols. My friends and I were given small wrapped gifts. Mine was a razor. The food bearers returned, urging us to take seconds. I was afraid to rise out of my chair and look around the room, lest this magic spell be broken, but I did, and confirmed that this was indeed a Christmas party and that the four of us were the only boot camp recruits dressed in olive-drab fatigues celebrating among perhaps a hundred people—men, women, and children—looking festive in their party best.

The evening ended in a melodious chorus of *Silent Night*. We had been there two hours. The lights came up and with eyes glazed like ornaments we followed our hostess to the front door, where our sergeant met us. I was so numbed by the experience I failed to thank her, but in the car there were several questions for the sergeant. He answered them all.

He said we shouldn't be so distrustful. He said the officers' wives threw a Christmas party every year for their friends and families and wished to invite a few boot camp soldiers far from home.

Why us?

Just lucky, he said.

Back at the barracks, behind a dopey grin, I thanked him for volunteering us and he replied, "Merry Christmas, Field. Sleep well." And I did. Visions of sugar plums and the whole bit. The curse at the start of the evening had vanished. And it wasn't the medicine in 12-ounce cans I had to thank.

Preconceptions are hard to ignore, but they're usually wrong. Fear is the worst. And Christmas gifts can surprise us, with wrappings that don't reveal the cheer to be found inside. A gift from strangers on my first Christmas away from home didn't cure me of foregone conclusions forever but taught me to expect surprises once in a while. And my friend was probably right. In the Army, volunteering will get you into trouble, though I never found out.

Yes, Charlie, There Is A Santa Claus

2002

My six-year old asked me the other day if Santa Claus was real or made-up. After careful thought, I replied, "Real, of course." Then I asked Charlie if *he* thought Santa was real, and he said yes.

"And how do you know he's real?" I asked.

"Because you wouldn't lie to me, Dad".

Parenting requires an occasional bout with guilt.

There are two ways children think of Santa Claus. Either they believe in the old guy, or they *say* they believe when they really don't. All kids, at some age, walk the thin line between the two and after a struggle with the potential consequences cross from one side to the other. Eventually, they let go of Santa completely and delight in the discovery that nothing has changed with the release, that Christmas still comes, but with a higher, more charitable purpose. It's a birthday party for Jesus, a birthday party where every kid still gets presents. As parents we don't try to rush this passage. Instead, we delay it as best we can, succumbing to nostalgic memory to recall dearly our own struggle and crossing.

I was eleven when I made mine. I was still sending letters to Santa, while secretly questioning the practicality of postal routes to the North Pole. And when I peered out my bedroom window and counted rooftops and multiplied the sum by all the cities in the all the countries in all the world, I concluded that there were far too many chimneys for the man to squeeze through in one short night, even taking into account changes in time zones. Despite these doubts, without any hard physical evidence to the contrary, I would go on believing for another year. Too many toy presents were at stake.

The year I turned eleven my grandparents came to visit us for the holidays. As was the custom when we had overnight guests, I gave up my bedroom and crossed the hall to bunk with my brother. On Christmas Eve, we climbed into bed anxious for morning. In whispers we shared our expectations of great presents. We played games in the dark. We traded sides of the bed a dozen times. When we finally wore the batteries out in our flashlight, we decided to call it a night and try to go to sleep.

It was late but the grown-ups were still downstairs. Their voices mixed softly with the melodies of Christmas music on the radio. The sounds were soothing and familiar, like every Christmas Eve. I remarked to my brother—four years my junior—that Santa doesn't enter a house if the grown-ups are still up, so Mom and Dad better get Granddad and Grandma to bed pretty soon.

We lay there is the dark listening. Then, suddenly, mixed with the music, there was a new sound, one I had never heard before. It was a soft irregular tapping, like hoof beats alternating slow and fast—tap, tap… tap…tap, followed by long periods of silence. My brother and I crawled from the bed and lay by the door to listen better. After each interlude of silence, the sounds would start again. The cycles repeated, over and over. Like the horse was starting and stopping.

The sounds came from the basement, two floors below, and sometimes were punctuated by the voices of my father or grandfather speaking in numbers. But they offered no other clues to the mystery.

Eventually, the sounds stopped for the longest time and were replaced by footsteps on the basement stairs. My brother and I dove back under the covers and pretended to be asleep. The lights downstairs went out and the footsteps came up to the bedroom level. A few minutes later the house was completely dark, and we let the mystery go and drifted off to sleep.

In the morning we rushed downstairs to find the presents Santa had left under the tree. I got a cap pistol and a model airplane. My brother got a baseball glove. It was a great Christmas.

As we gleefully leapt from present to present, my father walked over to the table at the end of the couch and picked up a piece of paper.

"Hey," he said, "Santa left us a note." He kneeled and we rushed to his side and read over his shoulder.

"Yeah, that's Santa's handwriting all right," I said confidently.

My father read. "Thanks for the cookies. I left a present in the basement. It was too big to put under the tree. Santa."

"Well, what do you know?" Dad said.

We didn't run downstairs; we *flew*, hardly touching the steps. In the basement we turned on the light.

There, before our eyes, in the middle of the floor, was a brand spanking new ping pong table. Our eyes grew big like little white plastic balls. We reached for the paddles and a ball.

Arriving a few seconds later, my father remarked, "Boy, old Santa sure was good to you guys this year. Imagine. A ping-pong table."

My brother took a swipe at the ball. *Tap.*

It bounced over the net and across the table top.

Tap, tap, tap…tap….tap…

Seized by an uncertain fear, I let the ball go by. *That sound!* I froze. The room went dark for me.

"One to nothing," my brother cried.

In silent horror I watched a scene play out on a screen in my mind: my father and grandfather, late the night before, down here in the basement, pulling a large box from behind the furnace….

No, I thought, it can't be.

"Pick the ball up," my brother said.

I shuddered in disbelief. But I kept my thoughts to myself. My brother looked at me with annoyance. Then, the hard look slid from his face and bewilderment took its place. His expression began to change in stages. First, his brow creased. Then, his eyes narrowed. When his mouth fell open, I knew that *he knew.*

We continued to play, our eyes from time to time lasering on each other. We both knew what the other was thinking.

After breakfast he and I went back to the basement by ourselves and whispered. We made a solemn pact, a pinky swear, to never, ever reveal the secret we had learned that morning. The truth was shocking, but we knew that the gifts of Christmases to come were at stake. If our parents knew that *we* knew, our letters to Santa pleading for toys would be ignored. It would be socks and underwear forever. What would Christmas become? We couldn't imagine.

We vowed to remain calm and returned upstairs.

"Gosh, Dad," I said. "Santa must've had a second sleigh to carry a big present like a ping-pong table all the way from the North Pole."

My father nodded in agreement, but with a hint of a smile at the corners of his mouth. Did he know that *we* knew? Or did he dwell in fantasy like us? Was he merely proud of himself for fooling his kids another year? Either way, I think he was just pleased watching his kids confront the mystery.

And so, with the passing of a generation, it is my turn. *I* assume my father's role in this timeless tradition.

Yes, Charlie, there *is* a Santa Claus. Last year, as your mother was putting you to bed, he fell in a snow bank outside your window while shaking a set of reindeer bells. This year I am giddy watching you prepare for his arrival. Be joyous, son. One year, but not this one, you will cross a line and figure out for yourself that Christmas is not what you thought it was but it still lives with all its wonder on the other side. It will still come, but it will be better than before. Trust me. You'll know Christmas as I do, as a birthday party where everybody *but* the birthday boy gets presents. You'll ask if it's Jesus' birthday. And I won't have to lie to you.

I'll Be Home For Christmas

2003

We always go home for Christmas. Every year. All of us. Every year we make a journey there, even if we don't cross our doorsteps. Without leaving our houses we gather our families in close and make spiritual journeys to where old traditions and memories are kept, to where we feel comfortable, warm, and loved. We *feel* a homecoming.

The distance we travel is greater than we think. Bethlehem was the site of the first Christmas homecoming and the guests who traveled to the manger that night started something. The wonder and joy they felt became their legacy to us, as well as their need for a pilgrimage to experience it. And so we too must travel to find Christmas. We go home in our hearts. Christmas and home are two words that sound wonderful together in the same sentence.

When I was a kid my family seldom travelled for Christmas, but every year we felt a warmth at home that wasn't there the rest of the winter. After I went away to college and came home for Christmas the first time, the warmth was even greater. The simplest decorations and traditions of all the past Christmases became special to me. Our house had always been home, but I felt a connection like never before, even after we moved one year to a new address.

One of our traditional decorations was a "spiritual" Christmas home. Not a real home, it was one of those model Snow Village houses that people collect in nostalgic little towns with depots and livery stables. My family had just one piece from the set, a two-story Victorian home with windows lit up by the glow of a single interior bulb. A bad electrical contact Dad was never able to fix made the bulb blink randomly, so that the house looked like there was a mad scientist busy in the basement. Every year we laughed about it. *Frankenstein, not frankincense, this year.* Still, when it was on display during the holidays, sitting on the fireplace mantle or on a shelf, the little plastic house evoked warm memories of our past Christmases, even though it didn't resemble any house we had ever had. We moved several times when I was young, but the little house followed us everywhere. It was a Christmas fixture for us.

One year while I was away at college, in the busy weeks that separate Thanksgiving and Christmas, my family moved. It was not a long-distance move, but from one house to another in the small town in eastern North Carolina where we had lived for two years. As Christmas drew near, I looked forward to renewing old traditions in a new house I had never seen. I imagined it from descriptions in my mother's letters.

I made plans for my homeward journey just a few days before Christmas. It was a 200-mile trip, and, for reasons of cheapness and adventure, I decided to ride my thumb, rather than Greyhound, and hitchhike the distance. I was certain it would take no longer than four or five hours relying on the kindness of strangers along the way. So I called home and told my mother to expect me by mid-afternoon.

Hitchhiking was popular with the youth of that era. Kids with long hair in bell bottoms and buckskin jackets were a common sight on interstate ramps and highway shoulders. My homecoming would take me through the conservative, rural south. So, on the morning of my journey I dressed in a buttoned-down shirt and tie and sport jacket. I felt this Joe College look would convey trust and politeness to the local gentry, thus improving my odds at getting picked up and having a swift journey. So, with suitcase in hand and a roadmap in my pocket, I wished my roommate a Merry Christmas and walked away from campus to stand on the edge of Highway 70 in Durham and begin my Christmas homecoming. It was a warm, blue-sky day, and I didn't wear a topcoat over my sport jacket.

I stuck out my thumb. Four cars whizzed by. The fifth pulled over. The journey began.

In the first two hours I covered almost a hundred miles, catching rides easily from businessmen, some dressed like me. They carried me eastward out of Durham and through Raleigh and past the suburbs on the capital's east side. I saw decorations for the season everywhere. I felt joy in the air. I applauded myself for my sport-jacket-and-tie decision. It was a glorious day. At one point I entertained myself singing with my thumb out.

A travelling salesman picked me up in front of a strip mall, drove fifteen miles, and dropped me off out in the country at the intersection of two narrow roads. He bid me good luck and turned off my route. After he was gone I sensed a quiet peace to my surroundings. The horizon was furrowed with grain silos and barns. I heard a rooster in the distance.

As I stood on the gravel shoulder and peered down the long stretch of empty blacktop to the west, I suddenly realized something. Actually, it was two realizations, neither reassuring.

One was that traffic for the rest of the trip would be light. The big cities and busy highways were behind me and ahead lay a landscape of quiet little towns separated by great distances. Still, half of my journey was done and there were hours of daylight ahead. The time of day—early afternoon—calm me a little.

But there was a second awakening.

I had mistakenly left the address and phone number of my new home in the desk back in my dorm. I had never seen my new house, now I didn't even know where it was. All I could remember was the name of a street. I shook off this preparation error and assured myself that all would go well, that once I got into town and found the correct street I would have plenty of daylight left to examine yards and mailboxes for clues to find the right house. Besides, *that* problem was a hundred miles away. My current situation was more pressing.

I waited the longest time for the next car.

It was a pick-up. My thumb was out as it approached and slowed down. To my good fortune, it rolled to a complete stop on the roadway. Inside was an elderly couple. I smiled and picked up my suitcase and took a step forward. The couple examined me suspiciously and then turned to speak to each other. Without a word, the man behind the wheel hit the gas and the truck sped away faster than it had arrived. Ten minutes later a car passed in a similar manner. Then a 2nd truck, and another car. Everybody was looking, but nobody was stopping. My good spirits of the morning turned to gloom.

As another car passed, leaving me in a cloud of exhaust as blue as my sport jacket, I yanked off my tie and stuffed it in my pocket. It occurred to me that in rural North Carolina a jacket and tie any day of the week but Sunday was a peculiar sight that could stir distrust and identify you as a suspected Yankee. Joe College on the side of the road was not a familiar sight in these parts.

A half-hour later, *finally*, someone picked me up and I was moving eastward again.

"You're not from around here, are you?" the driver noted.

I was about to be, I thought, if *you* hadn't shown up. I made a poor attempt at polite conversation. In seven hours I had only six rides. I had spent five of those hours standing still.

I was still sixty miles from home when the sun set. My ninth ride never reached 3rd gear and took me only as far as the next mailbox. "This is where I live," the driver drawled, turning into his driveway after having carried me only 200 feet. He took a stack of Christmas cards from his mailbox and went inside the house. I was still standing there, next to the mailbox, 20 minutes later when he turned on his Christmas lights. Through his storm windows I heard Andy Williams singing *Joy to the World*. My parents had that album. I started thinking about shepherds and wise men and wondered how far they had to chase *their* eastern star. I discovered that while Carolina winter days can be pleasant, the nights had a bite to them. I shivered in my thin sport jacket, reminding me again what a bad choice it had been.

The tenth ride was my longest and left me near the bright lights of a filling station. I sang the words to a country song that was popular at the time:

All God's children get weary when they roam,
Don't it make you wanna go home.

It was after 8 p.m. My eleventh ride was my last, from a school teacher who lived in my hometown and dropped me off at the end of the street that was my only link to my new address.

I strolled down the dark street, past a dozen houses. Everywhere drapes were drawn and porch lights were on. The neighborhood was silent, settled-in, peaceful as a manger. My hopes rose and fell at what I thought were familiar sights: the family car or my old bike in a carport. Is *that* my new home? No, no, keep walking. Perhaps I should knock on any door and…then I saw it.

It was small compared to the picture window in which it was framed. But it was like a lighthouse leading me to port, the randomly flashing light of a tiny box-like object on the window sill, a recognizable memory from my Christmas past. I let out a cheer and began to run. All the anxiety and discomfort of the trip vanished.

I opened the front door and the family dog leapt upon me. I dropped my suitcase. There was a single place setting on the dining room table waiting for me. Familiar voices and the smell of a fireplace told me my journey was over. I was home for Christmas.

The Christmas Program

2004

Ah, the wonders of Christmas Eve. The Eve holds a special magic compared to the big day to follow. It is the night or nights, the anniversary of the starlit event that gives reason for celebrating in the morning. And its calendar placement is at the absolute height of holiday excitement, arriving in a holy crescendo as advent and its growing sense of *he is coming* peaks and Christmas finally arrives with its declaration of *he is here.*

The night is so familiar to us, filled with ritual and tradition, but it can still bring new possibilities and mysteries. My curiosity is stretched to its absolute limits when I think of the shepherds arriving at the manger that first Christmas Eve. What were their thoughts upon arriving? When did they know what they were seeing? Besides the simple love of a mother and her child, did they know they were witnessing something special, a once-in-a-lifetime event, the birth of all the love of the world? And every year on the anniversary of that night did they search the heavens for another guiding star? It happened once, maybe it will happen again.

Every Christmas Eve I look for a sign that will keep me connected with the wonder of the first Christmas. I have expectations that the night will surprise me with something magical. I'm on a constant lookout for *my* guiding star.

When I was twelve I thought I saw it. Something happened to me at Christmas that year that convinced me signs of its wonder are all around us and all we have to do is keep our eyes open to see them.

That year—the year I was twelve—Christmas Eve fell on a Sunday. Besides a morning worship service and a candlelight service that night at the Second Presbyterian Church in Alexandria, Virginia, it was the day of the children's Christmas program at church. It would be a busy day.

The events that transpired that day actually had their beginning weeks before, on a Sunday morning in early December when my mother drove me and my brother Michael to church for our first program rehearsal. The route took us past the drive-in theater, which had been closed since October. That's what the marquee was supposed to say. I had gotten used to reading **CLOSED FOR THE SEASON** in individually arranged letters on the board. But I also knew that vandals with unique wordsmith skills often entertained passing motorists by rearranging the letters into anagrams with bizarre messages. On that particular Sunday the letters read:

SHARES COLD FEET SOON.

Created from a limited alphabet, the message, like many before, lacked precise meaning, although over the summer I had learned that *Lilies of the Field* held a secret dirty word. I never learned the identity of the authors. I thought they were clever.

At the church that day thirty kids were assigned roles in the program. This would be my fifth and last program, and over the years my parts had grown steadily in importance, starting as a simple wise man and moving up through the cast to where this year I felt qualified to play Joseph, the lead male role and the character with all the good lines. My excitement overflowed as I entered the church that December day.

But an hour later I was disappointed to learn that I was not to play Joseph, but rather, for the second year in a row I was to be the innkeeper, a supporting character with one simple line, when he tells the weary travelers that the inn is full. And I was completely devastated when Mrs. Young, the program director, announced that the coveted part of Joseph would be played by my brother Michael, in only his second program and who the year before had been a speechless and almost invisible shepherd. As we drove away from the church, Mom and Michael celebrated, while I sat in the back seat and pouted in cold silence.

That night we had company for dinner. Uncle Sam and my cousins came over. We would be *his* guests on Christmas Eve.

Sensing my gloom, Uncle Sam attempted to cheer me up with a joke. He was born and raised in Virginia at a time when it still had its roots in the Deep South, and he had the accent to prove it. With a slow, halting rhythm, his speech sounded like it had dropped the reins and climbed from the furrows.

"Did you hear about the Southern belle," he drawled, "that was being shown a home for sale? The realtor told her, 'This is a house without a flaw.' To which the belle replied, "Well, then, whatcha' all walk on?'"

Uncle Sam had a million of them.

As the weeks passed, my mood lightened. By the morning of Christmas Eve, just hours before the program, I was still reciting my single line with gritted teeth, but, as I listened through the wall to Michael practicing his lengthy part with confidence, I began to realize that perhaps he made a better Joseph, and that as the innkeeper I had reached my thespian peak. It *was* possible. Gradually, my anger lessened and I began to feel pride for my brother, as well as an acceptance of my own supporting role. The feeling warmed me to the point that I was about to enter Michael's room and offer words of support.

Then the anger returned.

We attended worship in the morning and then returned home for lunch. The program would begin at four.

On our way back to church I devised a plan for revenge. My single line, if modified just right, could bear more weight in the program than all of Michael's lengthy recital. At the same time I would test his ability to think and act on his feet.

We arrived and dressed in our costumes and took our places off-stage. Angels and shepherds were put in their places. The program began. The narrator told us that the world would be taxed. And Joseph and Mary began their journey to Bethlehem. At the entrance to the Bethlehem Inn, I took my position and waited.

When the storied couple approached and Joseph stepped forward to ask me if I had a vacant room for the night, I veered from the script and answered him with a bold wave of my arm, "Sure. I got *lots* of rooms. Come on in. Take any one you like."

The audience was hushed. Michael blinked quizzically. Recovering at once, he looked past me and examined the front of the cardboard inn with its painted door and windows and said, "Nah. This place is a dump. We're going to sleep in the barn instead."

And, as they say, the show went on, as it must.

The program concluded without any further improvisations. Afterwards, Mrs. Young looked at me with displeasure and then congratulated the entire cast. Michael punched me playfully on the arm.

The sky was still light as my father drove us from the church to Uncle Sam's. I sat in the back seat and wondered whether or not my stage improvisation had been a bad idea. I admitted to myself it was a mistake. Still, I thought hard about whether or not an apology was in order.

We drove past the drive-in theater. Nobody in the car paid attention to the marquee, except me.

As it slid past my window, I read it.

The wordsmiths had struck again, this time with a message that chilled me.

FIELD CHOOSES NOEL STAR.

I was stunned by its personal note. How did they know my name? What noel star? Then I counted the letters. Where did they get the extra two letters? I was about to say something but my voice stuck in my throat. I looked at my brother and Mom and Dad. They stared at the road ahead with blank expressions. They had not seen it. Had I imagined the personal message?

The words were still echoing in my head after dinner, when I went outside in Uncle Sam's yard with my cousins to pretend we were shepherds watching over the family dogs at night. The sky sparkled with hundreds of tiny points of light. I focused on one bright star in particular, shining above the trees to the east. I thought it was a sign, my noel star. I had a fleeting sense of the wonder of Christmas Eve and its revelations. Jesus was born in a manger. The story is retold year after year, but every year it is like new, as we all play key roles in the telling, shepherds and innkeepers alike. No role is more important than another. I felt my guilt lift off my shoulders.

I went inside to issue my delayed apology. Michael punched me in the arm and went back to playing a game of table hockey against our cousin.

Uncle Sam had arranged a nativity scene above his fireplace. Tiny figurines gathered around the baby Jesus: sheep, shepherds, an angel, the whole cast. Something odd-looking drew my attention, so I came closer and was surprised to discover that the wise men were wearing red firemen's helmets.

"Uncle Sam, there were no firemen at Jesus' birth," I said, overlooking that earlier in the evening *I* had attempted to re-write history.

Uncle Sam drawled, "Yes, there were. The Bible says so. It says the wise men came from afar."

Where Have All the Shepherds Gone?

2005

***

Here's a job listing you're not likely to find in the classifieds.

Wanted: A good shepherd. Must be willing to spend long hours alone caring for a flock. No fear of wolves. Nighttime work required. Must supply own staff.

Many occupations have come and gone in the last two thousand years. We don't need blacksmiths anymore. Or chariot drivers or clock winders or moat cleaners. Or, so it seems, shepherds.

Which is too bad because there is something special about shepherds. We associate them with only the best human qualities: duty, patience, safekeeping. Their work is peaceful and uncomplicated, in pastoral settings with lots of big sky and fresh air. There is time for creative thought and reflection. And there's usually a good dog for companionship.

But where are all the shepherds these days? Who's hiring them? What happened to them? *Somebody* has to look after the sheep. Are they victims of downsizing? Did advances in technology take their jobs away? If so, what technology? Fences?

There's a Shepherd College in West Virginia. Nestled in the Blue Ridge Mountains, overlooking the scenic Shenandoah Valley, it looks like a place where you'd expect to find grazing animals. It's beautiful, a slice of heaven. But there's no Animal Herding Department and no degree to be earned in shepherding. You can't even find an elective course in the subject.

I'm concerned about the endangered status of shepherds not because I think society needs more of them but because I don't want to break our link with their Biblical importance. We don't know the names of the shepherds in the Christmas story but we know the significant role they played. While tending their flock under a starry sky on the night of nights, they were visited by an angel with news that the Son of God was born that night in Bethlehem, where they went to share the angels' news with Mary, thus securing their place in the story as the first bearers of the good news: *for unto us, a child is born.* Mary may have pondered this in her heart, but the shepherds shouted it from the highest mountaintop. Can you blame them? Until that night, nothing exciting had ever happened on the job.

They were the original shepherds, chosen by God over fishermen and farmers and several other vocations to spread the joy. He must have had a reason to pick them. I suppose it was because shepherds have the time do a lot of star-gazing and are more likely to spot one dancing in the sky like the tail of a kite. But whatever the reason, ever since, when we speak of shepherds, we think of Christmas and regard them as sentinels keeping a vigil over something more important than a herd. And that's why I miss them. If Jesus returns, I want a shepherd to break the news to me.

If you Google "shepherd" on the internet, you'll get close to 5 million hits, but most sites use the word to mean something other than the original occupation. German shepherds have more web sites than real shepherds. What is interesting, though, is the great number of sites that give shepherds a contemporary meaning that answers the question, "Where *have* the shepherds gone?" They haven't gone anywhere. Shepherds are very much alive today, in numbers greater than ever, watching over flocks that stand on two legs. God has hired them to look after His work and tend to His children. Keeping faith with their Biblical tradition, they celebrate Christmas every year by announcing the same great news of joy as the original shepherds, *for unto us, a child is born, who will bring us goodness and light. We* are the shepherds now.

A Google search will yield countless references to "good shepherd", as if there is only one kind. What's more, there's something else to be found on the web, several variations of the same shepherd joke, one that reminds us how relevant shepherds are in our modern, busy world.

It goes something like this.

A shepherd was tending his flock in a remote pasture when suddenly a dust cloud appeared on the horizon, approaching at high speed, out of which emerged a shiny, silver BMW. The driver, a young man in an Armani suit and alligator shoes stepped out of the car and asked the shepherd, "Hey! If I can tell you how many sheep you've got, will you give me one?"

The shepherd looked at the man and then glanced at his peacefully grazing flock and answered, "Sure."

The driver turned off his engine and took some equipment from the back seat. He plugged his Blackberry into a laptop computer. He briskly surfed a GPS satellite navigation system on the internet and initiated a remote body-heat scan of the area. He used his phone to download additional information which he then beamed to his laptop via an infrared port. He turned on a wireless portable laser printer which produced a hundred pages of data. Reading from the cover page, he announced, "You have exactly 1,587 sheep."

"Impressive," said the shepherd. "One of my sheep is yours."

He watched the man carefully select an animal and bundle it up in the back seat of his car. Then he asked the man, "If I can tell you what your occupation is, will you give me my sheep back?"

Pleased to be a fellow sportsman, the man replied. "You're on."

"You're a consultant," the shepherd said, without hesitation.

"That's correct," the man said. "How did you guess that?"

"Oh, it wasn't a guess," the shepherd said. "What else could you be? You drive into my field uninvited. You ask me to pay you for information I already know and answer questions I haven't asked. And you know nothing about my business. Now give me back my dog."

Friends You Choose

2006

There once was a television program called *I'll Fly Away* about a family living in the South during the years of the Civil Rights Era, something I could relate to, having grown up in Virginia during that era. Of all its episodes, one was special to me.

In the winter of 1962, Nathan and Paul were best friends and high school wrestling teammates. The sport was the glue of their friendship, keeping them together despite many ways their lives were different.

They lived at opposite ends of town in neighborhoods that shared nothing in common. While Nathan's father practiced law for a living and was supportive of his children, Paul's father had a habit of breaking the law and beating his only son. The wrestling mat in the gym wasn't the only place Paul got to practice his combative skills.

Their love for wrestling didn't always apply to their coach. An ex-Marine sergeant who had fought in the Pacific, Coach Weed treated his wrestlers the same way he had led men into battle, barking orders and keeping a distance between himself and those he commanded. He viewed wrestling just as he had viewed war: a test of conditioning and courage. He was a bachelor who never spoke of family. Wrestling was his life.

Christmas fell in the middle of the wrestling season, and with his team contending for a championship, Coach Weed refused to let the holiday interfere with scheduled workouts.

"I want all of you here tomorrow morning at oh-nine-hundred," he announced after Tuesday's practice.

"But coach," Paul replied, "tomorrow is Christmas Eve."

"You have a problem with me, Slocum?" Coach asked. "There is no Christmas Eve on my calendar. No Christmas Day or Hanukah or New Year's. There are only two events on my calendar. Winning...and not winning."

Nathan whispered to Paul, "Scrooge. And we're the Cratchetts."

Nathan's family celebrated Christmas Eve every year, while Paul usually spent the day alone. But this year the boys planned to earn a little money during the day delivering poinsettias for a local florist, a job for which they had to swallow their wrestlers' bravado. So, after a particularly tough practice at which Coach Weed outdid himself in meanness, they showered and dressed and began their rounds, working through lunch to make up for lost time and finishing by late afternoon. When they were done, they were surprised to discover they had one extra poinsettia. Rather than returning it to the florist shop, Nathan suggested they deliver it to Coach's house, as a sort of peace offering.

"Yeah, but let's leave it on the porch," Paul added. "I don't know if I want to see him anymore today."

"Good idea. But let's not leave a note. Let's make him guess."

"Or we can write a note like it's from somebody else. The girl's gym teacher. Sayin' something like, 'I'd like to blow your whistle sometime.' That'll mess his mind."

They shared a laugh. Finally, they decided that the gift would remain anonymous.

They parked their truck across the street from Coach's house and walked up to his front door and were setting the plant on the doormat when, suddenly, the door opened and there was Coach, dressed in a bright green sweater and a red Santa Claus cap.

The boys froze in their footsteps.

"Bedford. Slocum," he announced above the sound of voices and music coming from inside his house. "What brings you my way?"

Cautiously, Nathan picked up the flowering plant and handed it to him.

"Ah, the symbolic poinsettia," Coach said, taking the plant in both hands. "The green stands for everlasting life, the white for the Virgin Mary, and the red for the blood of Christ. Did you know that, boys?"

A half-dozen middle-aged men appeared from behind him to look over his shoulder, and without looking back, Coach spoke to them. "Gentlemen, these are two of my warriors, Bedford and Slocum. And boys, these are a select gathering of my closest friends." He introduced them one by one, and to each name he added a suffix, the name of a battlefield or a warship or an island.

"How about some eggnog, boys?" he asked. "Smitty has won awards for his recipe."

Struggling for words, Nathan and Paul declined the invitation, with the excuse that the florist's truck had to be returned.

Above a chorus of "Merry Christmas" from the other men, Coach proclaimed, "Well, God rest ye merry gentlemen".

Back at the truck, Nathan asked Paul if he was dreaming. Paul was speechless. In silence they returned to the florist shop, said their good-byes, and headed to their separate homes. As he had expected, Paul found his house empty, so he put his coat on again and walked several blocks to Coach's house and knocked on the door.

Coach answered. "Slocum? What brings you back?"

"I thought I'd take you up on that eggnog, Coach."

"A wise decision," Coach answered. He led Paul into his living room, where several of his guests were seated at a long table wrapping presents. "Stay for dinner, Slocum," he said. "I have a turkey in the oven bigger than you." He rubbed the shoulders of one of the men at the table. "It's infused with Ridge's award-winning sage dressing."

"I don't want to intrude, Coach. And I know we've had our differences and all. Maybe you don't want me hanging around."

"Nonsense," Coach said. "Christmas is a time to remember not what divides us, but what unites us." He turned to the others at the table. "Gentlemen," he said, "one of my warriors will be joining us for dinner."

The man introduced as Ridge pulled back a chair. "Here, son. Have a seat and give us a hand."

"What's all this?" Paul asked, looking over a table covered with boxes and wrapping paper and ribbons.

"Toys for Tots," Coach replied. "Al here got us started in the program years ago. He was in the First Division. One of the lucky ones at Omaha Beach. If it weren't for him, we might be speaking German today." He tossed a doll in Paul's lap.

"Coach, I'm not much for wrapping presents."

"Do the best you can," Coach answered softly.

They stared at each other for the longest time. Finally, Coach broke the silence. "What? What is it, Slocum?"

"I dunno, Coach. I guess I never figured you for someone who liked Christmas."

Coach laughed, something Paul had seldom seen. "What's not to like? It's *Christmas*."

"You know, Coach, it's a...you know, a family thing."

51

"Ha!" Coach replied. "Family is like the cards you're dealt. You don't have to keep them. Friends," he said, motioning toward the men in the room, "say a lot about a man. Friends, you choose."

Smitty returned from the kitchen and handed Paul a glass of eggnog. "Here, son, drink up." Coach held up his own glass and said, "Glory to God in the highest, and on earth, peace among men." And then he and Paul toasted each other.

There is a true story about English and German soldiers fighting in Europe in 1914. On Christmas Eve, as soldiers on both sides rested in their trenches, a single German stood and began to sing. After he was finished, several lads on the British side answered with "God Rest Ye Merry Gentlemen". Then the Germans countered with a verse from "Stille Nacht". When the English joined in their own tongue, white truce flags were raised to the sound of a timeless Christmas hymn being sung in two languages. One by one, soldiers on both sides walked into No Man's Land to share brandy and chocolates and photographs from home. They played a flare-lit soccer game and decorated a lone tree with scraps of paper. At daylight they returned to their trenches. A similar story has been told about the Civil War.

Warriors have always celebrated Christ's birth in the most unholy places. Vietnam veterans will tear up listening to "Silent Night", as they remember singing it many years ago with two thousand of their comrades at a troop show in the jungle. Throughout history men trained for war have shown the greatest reverence for peace because they alone know what a great cost war extracts.

Christmas is a time for peace, when we remember not what divides us, but what unites us. It is not celebrated alone, but with the families we were born into and with the families we choose. At Christmas we are all one family.

Christmas Bell

2007

I have a friend, Phil, who several years ago suffered the unthinkable tragedy of losing his son in a swimming accident. Danny was a bubbly 6-year old, happy as Christmas, the day on which he was born, and his death sent Phil and his wife into a deep and prolonged grief that I can only imagine.

Phil sought relief by keeping himself busy. He worked long hours at his job as a traveling salesman and volunteered for community projects at every opportunity. When his church formed a committee for a building addition, Phil agreed to help.

Phil was assigned to work with the architect designing the addition. After reviewing several different plans, Phil was attracted to one that could be modified to include a bell tower. The architect replied that the addition of the tower still fit the church's budget, but without the bell, which would be quite expensive.

How expensive? Phil asked.

Thousands, 5-figure thousands, was the reply.

Still impressed with the idea of a bell tower and undaunted by the estimate, Phil chose the option and declared that he would purchase the bell himself and give it to the church as a memorial to Danny.

The project was scheduled for a late-autumn completion. Phil pledged to get the bell in time so that its first ringing could be on Danny's birthday, Christmas morning, in a special ceremony on the most special day.

He started by looking for a new bell, but was disappointed to learn there was only one foundry in the entire world, in a small town in Germany, that could cast a bell of the size and shape he was seeking. Including freight, the bell would cost twice the architect's estimate. And the waiting time was almost two years.

Phil chose not to place an order with the foundry but remained optimistic. When the architect asked what he should do, Phil answered, "Build the tower. I'll get the bell."

He began looking for a used one, making phone calls, sending letters, and searching the internet. He placed ads in newspapers and magazines. He grew tired hearing the same lame joke: "I hear there's a nice one in

Philadelphia, but it's cracked." He was advised to follow auctions and estate sales. Meanwhile, the church addition was built with a beautiful, but empty, tower. As Christmas came and went, Phil vowed to keep his promise to the congregation and to his son.

Then, the following spring, he got his first break. He learned of an upcoming auction in Milford, Wisconsin, a small town two hundred miles away, at which a bell of an appropriate size was to be auctioned. Phil drove to Milford early on a Saturday morning in April, only to discover that the bell had been removed from the auction the week before and purchased directly by a local resident.

Phil asked to see the bell and was given directions to a nearby farm. He drove there and parked his car on the edge of a highway at the end of a long, winding driveway. The bell was at their intersection, mounted on a pedestal of stone and wood. Phil was impressed by its austere beauty, and drawn to the engraved letters encircling it to spell out a biblical message, "For God so loved the world, that he gave his only begotten son…" Disappointed that he was deprived of a chance to bid on the bell, Phil got in his car and drove home.

Another Christmas passed. Phil's work often took him to Wisconsin and on one trip he passed through Milford and discovered that the bell was gone.

He drove up to the farmhouse and got out and knocked on the front door. He was met by a middle-aged man, the owner of the property, who informed him that after enjoying the bell in his yard for almost a year he had sold it to the local school board. It could be seen at the entry to the high school. Phil went there and found it on a brick foundation at the base of a flagpole.

Again, he drove home disappointed.

With no other opportunities to buy a used bell, he returned to Milford again and again with a curiosity about this bell he couldn't understand. When he was home, he thought about it often. Finally, on a trip through Milford one autumn day he steered into the high school lot and after spending a few minutes admiring the bell up close, he went inside.

He introduced himself to the school's principal and asked if he knew the bell's history. The principal politely said that he didn't. "But the village librarian," he said, "she's been around longer than I can remember. She might know."

The librarian found evidence in her records that the Village of Milford had owned the bell 50 years ago.

He had come too far to give up. So, he went to the village hall.

Had the village been the bell's original owner, he asked the clerk? She didn't think so. The village owned it for only a year, but she thought the bell had once hung in the tower of the First Lutheran Church on the other side of town. Before heading home, Phil decided to make the church his last stop.

There, he met Pastor Lyle Fenwell, a tall, silver-haired man who proudly professed to having been a member of the church for most of his life. He had been baptized, confirmed, and married there, and after moving around the state to serve other congregations had returned to First Lutheran 25 years ago to become its head pastor in what would be his last call.

"What can you tell me about a bell?" Phil asked.

Pastor Fenwell leapt at the question. "The church had a bell once," he said. "In 1920, ten years before I was born, a bell was hung in the church's tower. I know. From age 6 to 16, it was my job to ring it every Sunday morning. Oh, I remember it well, those cold winter mornings, me in my mittens." As he spoke, his face widened with a proud smile.

Phil noticed that the church lacked a tower.

"Where was the bell placed," he asked?

"Well," Pastor Fenwell said, "that's the sad part of the story. There was a fire in 1947 and much of the original church was destroyed, including the tower. The church was re-built without a tower. The bell was undamaged but sold to the village. Then the village sold it. I don't know what happened to it after that."

Phil told him that the bell was nearby, at the high school, and for the second time in the conversation Pastor Fenwell showed surprise. Together, they drove to see it, and along the way Phil explained his interest in the bell and his quest to build a lasting memorial to his son. They got out and the pastor walked up to the bell.

"My, my," he said. "The memories.." His voice trailed off and his eyes teared up as he ran his hand over the words, "For God so loved the world.."

Then he straightened and expressed content that at least the bell was still in the village.

Phil thanked the pastor and said good-bye. They stayed in touch, even exchanging Christmas cards the following year. In the summer Phil drove to Milford and had dinner with the pastor and his wife. The pastor announced his intention to retire at year's end.

Phil was faced with a difficult decision about what to do next, whether to continue searching or to concede that a new bell cast from German iron would be just as nice. His search was entering its fifth year. Meanwhile, the tower at his church still stood empty. Maybe it was time to finish the project. He gathered specifications for the bell he would purchase, and on a November morning was ready to make a phone call to a factory in Germany when, instead, he answered a call.

It was Pastor Fenwell.

"Have you found a bell yet?" he asked.

Phil replied that he had not.

"Well, then, can you arrange to rent a flatbed truck next weekend?"

"Yes," Phil said. "Why?"

"Because the congregation of the First Lutheran Church of Milford has an early Christmas gift for you. They have purchased the bell from the school and would like you to have it."

Phil was speechless, so Pastor Fenwell spoke for him. "I think it's about time your church's bell tower was finished, don't you?"

Phil trembled as he tried to express what he was feeling in his heart. "I'll accept the gift on one condition," he finally said.

"And what is that?"

"That you be my guest on Christmas morning to be the first to ring it."

"I graciously accept your offer," Pastor Fenwell said.

The bell was placed in the tower two weeks before Christmas. The church bulletin on Christmas Day contained a story about the bell's history, including the role played by Pastor Fenwell. As Phil escorted the pastor and his wife into church, he asked, "What did I do to deserve this? What compelled your congregation to be so generous to someone they've never met?"

"Well, I feel like we're old friends," Pastor Fenwell replied. "But the real reason is what you intend to do with the bell. When you told me that it would hang in a church tower, I thought that's where it's belonged for 50 years, in a place just like where it started. It's going home. A little closer to heaven. It completes a circle, don't you think?"

Pastor Fenwell was directed to stand at the tower's base and given a pair of white gloves with which to clutch the rope hanging from above. His wife sat in a pew next to Phil and leaned over to whisper in his ear. "When the good people of First Lutheran asked Lyle what he would like for a retirement gift, he said he wanted his bell back."

Many journeys ended that day, not just Phil's. As the bell rang over and over, Phil's heart lifted. He closed his eyes and pictured in his mind hands pulling on the rope to create the wonderful sound he was hearing, but the hands he saw were not in white gloves; they were in mittens, the small hands of a child, a 6-year old sending a message across time and space to another 6-year old, connecting in a Christmas miracle.

O Holy Night

2008

I t's been said that the wise men invented Christmas giving. Their gifts to Joseph and Mary and the Christ child started it all. And because they were wise, we surmise that their gifts were wise, too.

Edna and Charlie Grimes raised a family in a modest house in a small Southern town. Years later, after their children had grown and moved away, they still lived there and kept many of the important Christmas traditions they had observed with their children. This was during the Depression, when traditions were kept as long as they didn't cost too much.

One of the traditions was that every Christmas Eve they hosted a dinner for Edna's sister Louise and her husband Eddie. Afterwards, they cleared the kitchen table and the foursome played pinochle until it was time to leave for the 10 o'clock worship service at the First Presbyterian Church. On their way to church they stopped at Evelyn's house—she was Edna's other sister—to pick up their gift from Evelyn, always the same, a loaf of fresh sweet bread she made every year from a secret recipe that she vowed never to reveal. The bread would be enjoyed Christmas morning, which was also part of the tradition.

This was after the town got power —*electrification* as they called it in the rural south—and while the foursome played cards they enjoyed listening to music on the radio. On Christmas Eve the local station WWJD shelved its usual bluegrass format to broadcast Christmas carols.

Edna and Charlie had slightly different views of Christmas. Edna's was from the front pew. For her Christmas Eve was magical, a night to relive the Biblical account of Christ's birth, while Charlie regarded it simply as the night before the day of a great feast. His connection to the original Christmas Eve came from listening to the carols on the radio. He waited to hear one song in particular, *O Holy Night*, recorded by the singing cowboy, Gene Autry, which made it the best Christmas song ever in his opinion. When Gene came on the radio, the pinochle stopped and Charlie got a faraway look in his eye. To guarantee the moment, he would call WWJD in the afternoon to request that the song be played early in the evening before Edna dragged him off to church.

Edna accepted Charlie's limited spiritual horizon, and he often teased her about her unyielding faith in Bible stories. For example, there was the one about Jonah.

"Did he really survive being swallowed by a whale?" Charlie asked her once.

"Of course," Edna replied.

"How did he pull off that miracle?"

"Well, he did it."

"But how?"

Edna said she wasn't sure, but some day, when she got to heaven, she would ask Jonah how it happened.

Charlie chuckled and asked, "What if *he* isn't there? What if he went to, you know, the other place?"

"In that case," Edna answered firmly, "*you* can ask him."

Edna always got in the last word.

But on Christmas Eve there was peace in their house as long as Charlie got to hear the cowboy sing *O Holy Night*.

One year the tradition took a peculiar turn. Dinner was done and the dishes had been cleared and the pinochle game began. They had been playing for an hour when Charlie began to fidget. It was getting late and WWJD had yet to play his song. Soon they would need to leave for church. Charlie's anxiety was so great that between hands he got up and went to the phone to call the station, but the party line he and Edna shared with neighbors was too busy with holiday yakking for Charlie to get through and he returned to the kitchen table complaining.

"Oh, hush." Edna said. "Just be patient. You'll hear your song."

But Charlie was not convinced, and after his 3rd attempt to call the station failed, he went to the front door and put on his coat and cap.

"And *where* do you think you're going?" Edna asked.

"To the radio station. I'll take care of this myself."

"But it's your deal, Charlie," Eddie said.

"You're being ridiculous," Edna told him.

"I'll be back in twenty minutes."

Then Edna got in the last words.

"Stop at Evelyn's and pick up our sweet bread, mine and Louise's. It'll save us a trip later."

Charlie turned on the car radio and listened as he drove to his sister-in-law's for the bread. The loaves were fresh, still warm, braided into wreaths and wrapped with red ribbons. They filled his car with the wonderful scent of a bakery. Then he headed east to the edge of town.

He knew where to find the station, out beyond where the houses ended and the cornfields began. At night its location was unmistakable. It sat directly beneath a tall transmitting tower crowned by a big white light brighter than any star in the night sky. The light could be seen from miles away. Up close, it shimmered and cast distinct shadows.

Charlie marched into the station and as the final verse of *It Came Upon A Midnight Clear* went out over the airwaves the radio host leaned out of the control room and pulled earphones from his head and nodded with certainty. Yes, Charlie, I didn't forget, I've got *O Holy Night* coming up shortly, don't you worry. And Charlie left.

He stood outside the station and squinted up at the light and marveled at its brightness. Then his eyes moved down the side of the tower, nearly invisible in comparison, until he saw something he hadn't noticed earlier. Just beyond the base of the tower there was a small campfire, and against its flickering orange flame Charlie saw the silhouette of a kneeling man.

Charlie's curiosity spiked. He knew everybody who lived in town and anybody who didn't. He looked around and confirmed he and the man were alone. He stepped away from the station and walked toward the tower and campfire, craning his neck to look up at the bright light as he drew near.

When he was close, the man turned and stood in a gesture of surprise. He greeted Charlie with a silent nod of his head.

Charlie nodded back.

He saw that the man was *not* alone, that a young woman sat behind him, close to the fire, a coat over her shoulders, her arms closed tightly around a baby. The baby was awake, its small arms and legs in motion.

It was Charlie's turn to act surprised. The entire scene was unexpected. He struggled with words to say, unsure why the man and woman were here, and where they had come from. But then he remembered stories he read in the papers and heard down at the general store, stories about people on the move, men and women, and children too, victims of hard times. The president said all we had to fear was fear itself, but, clearly, some people's fears were greater than others.

The stranger broke the silence.

"Look, we'll be gone in the mornin'. We just need to be here tonight. Tomorrow we'll find my brother and he'll put us up."

Charlie held up his hand, the gesture saying *there's no need to explain.* Then he made an offer.

"It's going to be cold tonight," he said. "I can give you a lift to your brother's if you give me directions." He looked again at the woman. Her coat had fallen open and Charlie had a better view of the child.

"No, we'll be fine, but thank you."

"It wouldn't be any trouble," Charlie said. When the man didn't reply, he turned his attention to the woman. "How old is your boy, ma'am?" he asked.

"Three months. And it's a girl. Virginia."

"Sorry. That's a nice name."

"Named after my grandmother," the woman offered.

"It would be no bother," Charlie said to the man.

But the man's resolve, as well as his pride, was solid.

"Thank you for the offer, but we'll be fine.

"Or you're welcome to stay with me and my wife. We got plenty of room."

"We'll be fine here."

"Charlie nodded. The words "Merry Christmas" stuck in his throat. Even though he would have meant it, it wouldn't sound right. Instead, he held up his hand and said, "I'll be right back."

He went to his car and returned with the two loaves of sweet bread and handed them to the man.

"Please take these," Charlie said. The man accepted Charlie's gift gratefully.

Charlie said good-bye.

"Merry Christmas," the man and woman said together. Charlie waved in return.

On his way home, Charlie's mind was far away and he almost forgot to turn on WWJD. He was in the driveway when he remembered. Gene was singing.

Fall on your knees, Hear the angel voices,
O night divine, O night when Christ was born…

He sat in the car and listened until the song was finished. It touched him like never before. He wasn't sure why, just that he felt a connection between the song's words and his encounter with the couple under the station light. The words had always been special to him. But he never really *listened* to them until now.

He opened the car door and when the interior lamp came on he noticed something on the seat next to him. It was the church bulletin from a Sunday service of a couple weeks ago. On the front there was a picture of Christ and the words: "Just as you did it to one of the least of these, you did it to me. Matthew 25:40." The verse came from the Gospel lesson on the back of the bulletin, which he now read word for word.

Then he ran into the house.

"Well, mister impatience," Edna said as he rushed into the kitchen. "You missed your song. They just played it." When Charlie didn't answer, she asked, "Are you all right?"

Charlie said to no one in particular, "We should get going." Then he went to the hall closet.

"But it's only nine o'clock," Edna called to him. "We've got time for a couple more hands."

"No, we don't," Charlie said. "We need to stop at your sister's to see if she made a couple extra loaves of her top secret bread. That, or maybe we can pry the recipe from her, but I doubt it."

"Didn't you stop like I told you?" Edna asked, entering the front hallway.

"I'll tell you later," Charlie said, his voice coming from inside the closet. "Let's get going."

"We'll be too *early*," she said. "We don't want to get to church too early."

But Charlie didn't answer. He just handed her a coat. "Louise! Eddie!" he called.

"Charlie?" Edna asked. "What is the matter with you?"

Louise and Eddie appeared behind her, just as Charlie closed the closet door, his arms holding a wool bundle against his chest.

Edna asked him, "What on earth are you going to do with those blankets?"

Charlie got in the last words.

"Edna," he said. "Just *get* in the car."

This Little Light Of Mine

2009

When the Higgins family decided for the first time to put up outdoor Christmas decorations, it was the twins—Molly and Jack—who suggested a nativity scene, but not one with cardboard cutouts or stuffed dolls, but a *live* nativity scene in which the family would play the parts.

The twins were only six but knew all about the Christmas Story from Sunday School. Molly volunteered to be Mary and Jack claimed the part of Joseph. Mom and Dad would be shepherds and Baby Joe—just 5 months old—would play Jesus. Mom and Dad were excited, too.

The Higgins lived on a gravel road outside of town. They had no neighbors, except Mr. Thomas, a widowed dairy farmer a half-mile away whose several acres of pasture surrounded the Higgins on all sides. The twins had grown up accustomed to seeing cows grazing beyond the backyard fence. When they suggested the historical accuracy of their set could benefit from live animals, rather than fake ones, Dad asked Farmer Thomas if he could borrow something from his dairy herd and the farmer obliged him with a cow and several bales of hay.

Dad built the manger from scraps of lumber he scrounged from the garage. He plugged an extension cord into an outlet on the house and was connecting it to a trouble light when Jack declared that he wasn't familiar with any version of the Christmas Story mentioning the manger illuminated with electric lights. Jesus was born by the warm light of a fire or oil lamp, so Dad instead hung a propane lantern he bought at Target on one of the manger's posts. Mom made clothes for everyone from old blankets and bed spreads. When the cow and hay bales arrived, they were ready to put on their first show.

There wasn't much traffic on the Higgins' road, and at night no reflected light from town. Besides the lantern and a distant yard light from Farmer Thomas's place, the only lights were from above, a slice of the moon and a high ceiling of stars. Molly sat at the back of the manger next to Jack with her arms around her baby brother, who slept through the production. Mom and Dad stood in front clutching a rope tethered to the cow and marveled at the joy in the twins' faces, lit by the soft yellow glow of the lantern light. It was a magical moment for the family, even if only six cars passed the first night and nobody got out to admire the scene up close.

The crowd on the second night wasn't much better, when eight cars slowed while driving by. The poor audience was disappointing but didn't spoil the family's enthusiasm to stand under a starry sky and gain a sense of the holy wonder the angels and shepherds must have felt at the first Christmas. Nor did it dismay Molly and Jack from insisting that they stage the nativity scene again the following year. The production was repeated in every detail, except that Baby Jesus was a year older and fidgeted in his sister's arms.

After the second year Farmer Thomas stopped by the house one night to announce that he was retiring from farming. It was hard work, too strenuous for someone his age, and he had no choice but to sell the farm to a buyer who wasn't interested in farming but instead would divide the land's many acres into small lots and build houses to sell. The road would be paved and the Higgins would have neighbors at last. Farmer Thomas assured the Higgins they would still get a cow and hale bales at Christmas.

Twelve houses were built and occupied the following year. The Higgins met their new neighbors and everybody got along. But now there were streetlights and front porch lights to flood the night sky, and as the Higgins staged their third manger scene the neighbors strung multi-colored lights under their eaves and around windows and above garage doors. Most of the stars in the sky vanished. There were more passing cars, but no walk-ups, not even the new neighbors, to witness the nativity scene.

It was the folks across the street—the Brophys—who came up with the idea of a contest the following year, a contest to see who could stage the grandest display of Christmas lights and yard ornaments. The Brophys said it would create a community Christmas spirit, inspire creativity, and define the neighborhood as a place where everyone *really* knew how to celebrate the holiday. They arranged for the mayor of the town to be the judge.

"What do you think?" they asked. "Everyone else is on board."

Neighborly to a fault, Mom and Dad agreed to the contest, and Molly and Jack were okay with the idea as long as they repeated their nativity scene without any modifications, except that Baby Joe was now old enough for a two-legged part and looked forward to being a cow herder. His part in Mary's arms would be replaced by a plastic doll.

Before Thanksgiving that year the Higgins realized there were big changes coming. The neighbors started decorating in November. Their yards were cluttered with plastic Santas and upright candy canes and luminescent snowmen and strings of white lights arranged to spell "Season's Greetings". The winner of the first year's contest was the house with a giant star so high above the roof that it appeared to hang from the sky.

At the nativity scene, Mary and Joseph were now in the fifth grade.

Dad was feeling competitive and suggested the family try to win the contest the next year by adding wattage to their display, but the twins opposed the idea, and he backed down.

As the fifth Christmas of the nativity scene approached, there was evidence that neighbors were taking the contest too seriously. Cranes were brought in to erect decorations at great heights, and one family installed a second electric service and meter to feed its power-guzzling display. The predominant theme was motion, with motorized reindeer and elves and Disney characters with oversized heads frolicking on flood-lit lawns. The winner was a Santa's sleigh that started at the top of a thirty-foot artificial pine tree and descended to the ground at an angle on an invisible wire, while a robotic St. Nick waved from his seat atop a mountainous cargo of gift-wrapped presents. All night the sleigh went up and down, up and down, up and down...

More cars drove by. Word about the decoration contest had passed through town. That was nice.

But also that year, Joe learned that if he used two hands when holding the cow's rope, it didn't hurt so much when getting dragged.

In the sixth year, Dad strung a set of lights across the front porch but they mysteriously malfunctioned after the first night. Upon investigation, he discovered the string had been cut clean as if by a surgeon's scalpel.

"Squirrels," echoed the twins together. Mom said nothing.

Then the local paper announced it would send a reporter to cover the contest. On the night of the competition galaxies of colored lights synchronized to a cacophony of music filled the neighborhood. There were so many lights that shadows disappeared. One yard featured an alternative manger scene with a trio of Santas playing the wise men bowing before a gingerbread Jesus. The winning family built a railroad track that circled their house, with a black locomotive pulling two coaches and puffing smoke to steam-engine sounds blaring from hidden speakers. After each lap of the house the train stopped in front, where a mechanical boy standing in the snow asked, "Where you going?", and a life-like conductor leaned from the train to holler, "Why, the North Pole. This here is the Polar Express". The question and answer were repeated every 3 minutes.

That year, Joe learned not to stand behind a cow when she lifts her tail.

Then there was the seventh year. The Allens on the corner were out to win. While his neighbors raked leaves and put up storm windows in October, Mr. Allen began construction of what appeared to be a Ferris wheel, a complex structure of beams and struts bolted in the shape of a giant circle on its edge and supported on a massive hub turning atop a column twenty feet high. He mounted a hefty motor and gear reducer on the hub and pulled heavy wire through a buried conduit as thick as a fire hose. At night he could be heard in his garage cutting and welding pieces of steel.

One day a panel truck backed up in his driveway and dropped off boxes and boxes of light strings. It took a week to clip them to the wheel. Neighbors stood in the street and tried to guess the image the lights would create when lit.

Finally, the night of the competition arrived. As the grand displays of previous years came on one by one with their dancing reindeer and flashing stars and descending Santas and roundabout trains, Mr. Allen waited for the mayor and news reporter to arrive before going outside for the premiere of his yuletide spectacle.

The Higgins took their places in the manger scene, now featuring a goat. An avalanche of blinding white light from the other homes turned the pastoral intent of their display into a Las Vegas streetscape. Molly and Jack squinted into the glare, showing for the first time a look of displeasure. Molly was about to speak, when the unspeakable happened.

Down the street, with the mayor and reporters from TV and the local paper watching from the street, Mr. Allen stood at the control box he had mounted on the side of his garage and flipped a switch. Then, he looked up at the Ferris wheel with great expectation.

But he would never know if his creation was an award-winner. Nor would he know if the oversized service he had installed could deliver enough electricity to turn his giant wheel. It probably could. What wasn't big enough, however, was the capacity of a substation a mile away that powered the neighborhood—and most of the city as well—and in an instant the electrical demand of Mr. Allen's creation and all the other amp-sucking displays in the neighborhood threatened to overload the station and a major circuit broke open in self-defense. In the blink of an eye, every house and yard display and streetlight in the neighborhood went black. The sudden darkness even absorbed sound. The night became eerily silent.

Only one light remained, the lantern hanging in the Higgins' manger. The Higgins looked up to witness something they hadn't seen in years: their nativity scene in a completely dark landscape, peaceful under a dome of bright stars.

"Wow!" said Joe. This was the first time he had ever seen the manger this way. All the scenes in his memory were under floodlights.

The Higgins remained quietly in their places and marveled at the powerful silence of their simple display. They listened as front doors on the street opened and closed. Over the next several minutes they became aware of the neighbors leaving their powerless homes and crossing the street and walking along the curb and emerging from the dark to stand next to the manger.

Dad looked at his children's faces in the lantern light. Their eyes shined and their cheeks were rosy in the night air.

"Congratulations, Daddy," Molly said, clutching Baby Jesus.

Dad eyed his daughter curiously.

"We won."

White Christmas

2010

On Christmas Eve Tom comes home from work at noon to get ready for the family's trip to southern Iowa. His wife Sally has packed the car and their children Nikki and Mark are already in the backseat, comfortable in a nest made from blankets and pillows. They leave at two o'clock. Ahead is a five-hour drive to celebrate Christmas with Tom's mother in the house where Tom grew up.

Besides a trunk full of wrapped gifts, they are bringing with them a unique set of anxieties. Sally is uneasy about spending the next 48 hours under one roof with a platoon of in-laws. Tom worries about how his mother will hold up at the first Christmas since the death of Tom's father. Mark is eleven and struggles with the reality of Santa Claus and his capability of delivering Mark's presents, particularly when he is away from home. And Nikki is five going on six, or, as she puts it, the age when she will need both hands to tell people how old she is, and her private fear is that her grandmother lives too far south for snow, and what is Christmas without snow? Tom assures her there were many white Christmases in his youth.

Tom tries to comfort her with a story from his youth.

"Nikki, we'll be staying in the house where I grew up," he says. "I remember when I was your age, lying in my bed on Christmas Eve. There was a yard light outside my window and I could see the snow falling. The snowflakes looked big and thick and were floating, almost like they were feathers. Christmas snow is like that." Nikki likes the feather image but remains skeptical.

They arrive at seven o'clock. They are last to arrive. Tom's brother Dick and his wife and three kids have driven from Chicago and his sister Sue, divorced and living in California, has flown to Des Moines and rented a car with her two children. As Tom shuts off the engine, Nikki jumps out of the car and stamps her foot on the dry, brown lawn in front of her grandmother's house.

"I knew it," she says, sighing.

They are hungry and there is catching up to do with family but church starts in an hour so they leave after unpacking the car. Their family of thirteen occupies two rows of pews in the First Lutheran Church.

For the first time in forty years Tom's mother Carol is without her husband at her side, where Tom sits now. He remembers the last time he was in this church, on the day of his father's funeral, or, as Nikki called it, the day the angels came. Sunshine lit up the stained glass windows that bright summer day, but now they are decorated with wreaths and the church is candle-lit as the family sings timeless hymns and listens to the Christmas story. Tom smiles at the memories he has of First Lutheran, baptisms, and weddings, including his own, and the notion that three generations of his family are present this Christmas Eve.

Afterwards, they linger in the narthex, reconnecting with old friends. Tom shows his kids a framed photo of his confirmation class 20 years ago. Mark asks his father about a list of names engraved on an adjacent wall plaque.

"Who are they?" he asks.

"They're men who died in the service," Tom answers, looking for names he recognizes.

Mark whispers, "Why would people die in a church service?"

Tom explains and they both laugh.

Back at Carol's they eat a late meal of soup and sandwiches, after which the adults linger in the dining room while the kids scatter around the house. Carol announces the sleeping arrangements. The seven kids are put in Tom and Dick's old bedroom, the oldest five in blankets and pads on the floor, while Nikki and her four-year old cousin Martha take the twin beds. Dick and his wife will take the queen in what had been Sue's room growing up, Tom and Sally roll out a mattress on the floor of the sewing room, and Sue will sleep on the couch in the den. It all seems to work out nicely.

Tom stops in his old bedroom to say good night to the kids and finds Sue reading a book to them, *The Mitten*. He recalls the story, a folktale about a boy who accidentally drops a mitten on the ground in the forest and, magically, one-by-one, animals crawl inside the mitten in search of warmth and don't come out. The kids remark how large the mitten must be and are surprised by the artist's depiction of it, stretched enormously, but no doubt a bit crowded inside.

Then Sue's son laments that Santa Claus will go to his house in California and not know to bring gifts to Iowa. Tom glances at his own son, who appears puzzled as he wrestles privately with the Santa mystery. The grown-ups say good-night and turn out the lights.

At last, a moment Tom has been anticipating arrives. He sits in the den with his mother and asks how she's doing, but instead Carol wants to talk about tomorrow, and Tom realizes that Christmas is too busy, with too many people and too much going on, to gauge how someone is dealing with sudden loneliness.

Finally, as everyone turns in, Carol asks Tom for a favor, that tomorrow, at dinner, he sit at the head of the table, a peculiar request, but as long as Tom can remember it was his father's place and his duty to lead the family in grace and carve the ham. He knows the small task is terribly important to his mother, especially this year. "You're the oldest," the mother says to her son. "Besides, I've seen your brother with knives."

Everyone else goes to bed, but Tom stays up late. The entire house is dark as he sits by the light of the Christmas tree listening to choral music on the radio turned down low. He connects in spirit with the carols, and is comforted by the memory of his father listening to the same songs and the promise that his children will never grow tired of them either. He startles himself with an unexpected but pleasing thought, that he feels at peace here, that this house where his own Christmas memories began still feels like home, until he realizes that it's not the house but the gathering of family that makes him feel so good. He knows that it is the walls of the heart that make a Christmas home. Warmed by the revelation, he turns off the radio and unplugs the tree and goes upstairs to bed.

In the morning there is coffee and juice and sweet rolls followed by two hours of opening presents. Tom gets up from his chair several times to pull his mother from the kitchen and remind her that whatever it is can wait.

Dinner is at one. His brother Dick is about to sit at the head of the table when Tom directs him to a seat on the side.

"Howcum you're sitting there?" Dick asks.

Tom flaps his left arm and replies. "Southpaw. I don't want to bump elbows with anybody." Dick accepts this reasoning and nods his head and sits.

The meal is wonderful. Carol has seen to it that it is perfect, including the serving of a ham, which for years was a special Christmas treat for her husband. The dinner may be the last big event of the day and the family's celebration of Christmas, but Tom doesn't quite see it that way. He knows there is another holiday ritual about to begin, which is to fill the remains of the day with small but important goings on. It's a time for being together without having to do anything together. The kids try out their new toys while the adults gather to talk or play cards and then move apart to corners of the house only to find each other again. Dick watches a football game on TV in the den. Sisters-in-law plunk out duets on the piano in the living room and Sue joins her mother in the sewing room to admire her works in progress. As Tom takes a cup of coffee to the den to join his brother, he senses the closeness of everything. There may be spaces between family members all year long, but not at Christmas.

Mark sets his new I-Touch aside to sit by his father.

"Dad, I'm trying to figure something out," he says. "I don't know about Santa Claus and all that, but Christmas is like a birthday party for Jesus where everybody else gets presents. Right?"

Tom nods his head.

"That doesn't seem fair," Mark continues. "What does he get? What do we give him?"

Tom takes the long route in answering. "Well, our present to him might be that we care for each other. When we give presents, we're telling people we love them. As long as we never stop loving, we'll continue to give presents. Maybe that's all the gift Jesus wants."

Mark thinks before replying. "Yeah. Sure. I can live with that." Then he returns to his game.

Carol calls everyone together in the den. "I have special presents for everyone," she announces. She hands each of her three children a DVD box. "I had your father's home movies put on a disk."

Tom and Dick exchange looks of surprise.

"Well, don't just sit there," Carol says. "Let's watch."

Her husband was a video guy before the word was invented, filming everything in 8mm, from family vacations to baptisms, birthdays to first days of school. Now Carol has turned to modern technology to preserve the best part of their past.

"Sally, come see this," Tom shouts. They laugh reliving memories on the TV screen. When they come to the Christmas scenes, they watch Tom's father dressed as Santa Claus leaving the house with toys for all the kids in the neighborhood. Playing Santa was a father's role, he once told Tom. In close-ups his broad smile peeks from behind the clipped-on beard.

"Remember the year he fell off the roof?" Sue asks. Dick finishes the story. "He shook those reindeer bells so hard he slipped and fell in the snow bank next to the house."

The video ends. "Thanks, Mom," her children say. They get up to give Carol hugs as she wipes her eyes with her sleeve.

The last meal of the day is leftovers. Afterwards, Tom slips away and goes upstairs. He takes two soft pillows from the kids' bedroom and then climbs another stairway to the attic. It's chilly there. As a boy, he would look for hidden presents up in the corners of the attic, and as he rips open the ends of the pillows and then sets them carefully by the window he comes to realize that the best part of Christmas is its mix of memories and surprises, a day celebrated at a crossroads where old traditions are kept and new ones are about to begin.

At the end of the day he joins Sally and Carol in his old bedroom to say goodnight to the kids. He walks carefully between the blanket lumps on the floor to cross the bedroom and give Nikki a kiss. He thinks of *The Mitten*, and how the story speaks of his mother's house at Christmas, as she magically fits everyone in its limited space.

"Did everybody have a great Christmas?" he asks, and receives a medley of cheers. "Prayers are better in the dark," he says, turning out the light. He leaves and closes the door behind him.

The glow from the screen of Mark's handheld game shines off his face until Carol reaches down to take it from him.

"You've been playing this all day," she says.

"It's okay, Grandma," he answers. "It's wireless."

"So are prayers, young man," she answers sharply before sitting next to Sally on the bed.

At the last *Amen*, Nikki bolts up suddenly and points toward the window. "Look, it's snowing!" she exclaims.

Outside, big white flakes float in the glow of the yard light, a few at a time. The other children rise to their knees and shout with glee.

Sally tells her daughter, "I suppose this means your prayers were answered."

Nikki nods her head. Everyone is looking out the window, all except Sally, whose gaze is fixed on her daughter's face and a smile of such boundless joy it can be seen in the dark leaping from her face.

It is Grandma who finally speaks.

"The snowflakes look just like feathers, don't they?"

The Garage Singer

2011

*M*ake a joyful noise to the Lord, all the earth! *Serve the Lord with gladness! Come into his presence with singing!*

Ted knew this Bible verse by heart. It was partly why he joined his church's choir: to make a joyful noise for the Lord. He sang tenor standing in the choir's back row, an appropriate position for him. He knew that his love for singing surpassed his talent for it. While the pitch of others in the choir, including the tenors, could be bulls-eye perfect, his aim could drift and miss its mark a wee bit, akin to horseshoes and hang grenades where close enough was considered good enough. But that didn't stop Ted from wanting to come into *His* presence singing loud and proud.

Christmas music was what Ted loved the most. In particular he was attracted to Christmas choral music and its multitude of voices rejoicing Christ's birth in perfect harmony. It was a spiritual experience for him, with the lyrics evoking great scenes of the night when all the love of the world was born, with the star in the East, the manger, Mary and the child surrounded by shepherds and wise men, and angels looking down from above. Only music could capture the glory of that night of nights. Christmas was the reason God gave us music. A person just *had* to sing about it.

So, when the choir director rolled out the annual Christmas choral service by asking for a volunteer to sing the solo for *Comfort Ye My People* from Handel's Messiah, which had been written for a tenor, Ted heard two voices in his head, one urging him to make a joyful noise by himself and the other warning him to stay quietly in the back row, but Ted listened to the first and ignored the second and thrust his hand in the air. Everyone in the choir was surprised by his show of courage.

Ted had a unique musical tradition for celebrating and connecting with Christmas each year. He loved the songs of the season so much that in the glorious days of autumn he gathered a stack of his favorite Christmas choral CD's and placed several at a time in the tray of the CD player in the living room. Nearly every day for the next two months he would sing along with them.

His wife objected to the schedule of this ritual. She loved the holiday and the music inspired her, and her Christmas cheer was unmatched, but she believed ecclesiastically that there was a season for everything and that the Christmas season shouldn't start too soon. She knew it was diminished if stretched too long. Advent begins with snow of the ground, not leaves, so her rule at home was that Ted keep his music on the shelf until after Thanksgiving.

One night in early November she came home to find Ted singing along to *In the Bleak Midwinter* on the CD player, and she cheerfully ordered him to turn it off. November could be bleak but in no way was it midwinter.

"You can play your music *after* we put up a Christmas tree," she said.

"But we won't buy a tree until December," he answered.

"That's right. And that's when the season begins."

"But the season has already begun. Fleet Farm has had decorations up since Halloween."

"Fine," she said. "Then go to Fleet Farm and sing your heart out to the snow tires."

That gave Ted an idea. He filled a shoe box with CD's and unplugged the player and went out to the garage and set up a music station on the work bench. He threw a log on the wood burner, selected the music of *Messiah*, cranked up the volume, and hummed along to the overture. When the first solo began he tilted his head back and sang full-throated to the tools and rakes and garden hoses, "Comfort Ye...comfort ye, my people". His voice was sharpened by the unique acoustics that only concrete and drywall can create. Ted was in his happy place.

He practiced every day for a month, growing more and more satisfied with his version of the piece. Finally, the big day arrived—the first Sunday in December. After the call to worship and a gathering hymn, Ted stepped forward to stand by himself and sing.

He looked out over the congregation. He never knew the church could hold so many people. The piano accompanist played the introduction and four measures later Ted took a stab at the first note, singing the *come* in *comfort* on a dotted eighth note, which he knew made it some other fraction. He was pretty good at math.

Then he felt dizzy. His throat went dry and his knees buckled a bit. A bead of sweat formed on his brow. He was powerless to correct this sudden and unexpected state of unease. He plowed forward in song while uninvited thoughts crept into his head, destroying his concentration.

Actually, as he sang, there were four distinct thoughts ricocheting in his mind, and they did absolutely nothing to help his performance. Why they were in his head in the first place was a complete mystery.

First was the realization that singing to the congregation wasn't the same as singing in the garage. Stage fright.

Second, he missed the support of the other tenors, whom he was accustomed to hearing as he sang. He need a crutch.

And three—the weirdest thought of all—was that when he studied the music in his hands the many notes moving up and down on the staff reminded him of baseball. *Weird.* It was like he was at bat and the notes were well-thrown pitches from the mound, and like pitches they came in a variety of deliveries, all mixed up to surprise him, with different placements—some high, some low—and at different speeds, some like change-ups making you wait, and some—the eighth and sixteenth notes— like fastballs blowing by you and challenging you to catch them. Ted was swinging early, swinging late, and occasionally fouling one to the screen.

But the fourth thought was comforting and carried him to the end of the piece. It was the prayer the director had taught the choir to recite at the end of every rehearsal, with words that advised how to sing joyfully.

The prayer went like this.

"Lord, grant that what we sing with our lips, we may believe in our hearts, and what we believe in our hearts, we may show forth in our lives."

At that moment, as Ted readied himself for the last measure of breaking balls, he realized that he truly was singing words that he believed in his heart and what he believed in his heart he showed in his life. It's just that his lips were letting him down.

Finally he was finished, and slumping in embarrassment he returned to his place with the other tenors. As they were leaving the church his wife complimented him on his creativity. At home Ted headed to the garage. His wife said it was okay for him to bring his music into the house, but Ted waved her off. He fired up the woodstove and turned on the CD player. He chose *Messiah* and sang along. In his familiar place again, it sounded better.

Ted lost track of time, but while accompanying the *Hallelujah Chorus* he looked up and was surprised to see the choir director standing at the door. He welcomed her in and lowered the volume of the music. She thanked him again for his solo and Ted shrugged. Then, she got to her reason for being there.

"Remember the short story *Gift of the Magi?*" she asked. "Remember the gifts the couple gave to each other? The beauty of the story is that the couple didn't *have* much to give each other but that didn't stop them from giving what they had. The gifts they gave were part of them, their best part. Theirs were the greatest gifts of all."

When Ted didn't answer, she went on. "That is what Christmas gifts are meant to be. Thank you for your gift today."

Ted was a little confused but slowly came around and said, "You're welcome. But I should be thanking you."

"And I know how you can," the director said. "I'd like you to sing again on Christmas Eve, the same piece. Are you willing?"

What else could he say? "Of course. I'd be delighted."

"You'll be fine," she said. She gave Ted a hug, thanked him again, and said goodbye.

Ted stayed in the garage listening to his music and thinking about how well the day was turning out. And he thought about the lessons he had learned. He loved the music but more importantly singing was not just a message from the heart, it was a gift too, one to be shared. Finally, as he put the shoe box of CD's under one arm and the player under the other and headed back into the house, he had another baseball-is-like-music moment, and thought about how Nick Punto was no Killebrew but that didn't stop him from trying to get around the bases, and while none of us can sing like Caruso, or Phil Dahl, we should never stop making joyful noises.

No Room In The Inn

2012

Meet the modern family at Christmas. We can identify with the modern family. We feel busy and rushed. The demands of the season become a long shopping list.

✓ Parties
✓ Buy a Tree
✓ Decorations
✓ Gift Buying
✓ Greeting Cards
✓ Outdoor Lights

There is a need to schedule everything. Some travel is required. It seems that every year there are new events to place on the December calendar. We spend too much time shopping as we feel the tug of an evil commercial force. Easter has *Good* Friday but nowadays the Christmas season begins with *Black* Friday. Why is that?

The expression *Happy Holidays* has displaced *Merry Christmas* with too many well-wishers, and we know they aren't the same. Happy Holidays is an indifferent greeting, a noisy reference compared to the quiet peace and simple joy implied by Merry Christmas. The music of Happy Holidays reverberates in shopping malls and television ads and elevators. The good news of the Christmas Story is hard to hear when celebrating Happy Holidays. The hymns and carols remind us of this. Listen.

The world in solemn stillness lay to hear the angels sing.

Or,

Still, still, still, one can hear the falling snow.
For all is hushed, the world is sleeping
Holy star, its vigil keeping

There seemed to be more comfort and joy in traditional Christmases long ago, captured in Currier and Ives prints, or in old black-and-white movies. At least we want to believe that. We imagine going to the window to see carolers singing outside under a streetlamp while the house inside smells of gingerbread and evergreen. Or, we picture a brightly-lit department store window filled with toys, while kids on the sidewalk press their excited faces against the glass. Maybe Christmases were never like that, but we want to believe they were. Peace and simple joy. Where do we find it today? Or, if we don't know where to look, can it find us?

Let me introduce you to a modern family, a family just like all of us.

Jeff and Mary have two children, Dick and Jane, ages 11 and 8. Every year they are happy at Christmas, but the season still feels like a race that won't end until Christmas Day. On Christmas Eve, with the finish line in sight, there is one last hurdle for the family.

Jeff has to work during the day and won't be able to travel with the rest of the family to attend Christmas Eve dinner with Mary's parents, who live in a small town a hundred and twenty miles away. So, Mary will take the kids by herself to see her parents and then make the long drive home after dark. They've had to do this before.

After dinner Mary stays a little too late, lingering over the dessert with her parents. She wants to get home and put the kids to bed, but it is almost nine before she gets up from the dinner table to go. She packs her gifts in the car, hugs and wishes her parents Merry Christmas, and buckles the kids in the car. As she backs out of the driveway, it begins to snow in big, delicate flakes that would be lovely if she were sitting at home looking out the window without the need to drive someplace.

The kids succumb to the collapse that happens when a sugar rush and the excitement of opening presents wear off at the same time. Dick falls asleep in the back seat while Jane, strapped in the front, goes bobblehead. A second cup of coffee has given Mary the buzz she needs to be alert at the wheel. Most of the drive is on two-lane roads that wind through dark forests and quiet small towns with quaint names like Sugar Hill and Twin Mountain.

An hour into the trip, as the snow continues to fall, Jane straightens herself in her seat and says to her mother in a quiet, endearing tone, "Mommy, I have to go to the bathroom."

Mary assures her there is a gas station in the next town. Being eight, Jane trusts her mother and relaxes.

But the next station is closed. In fact, everything in the next town is closed so Mary drives on. "Mommy, I really—"

"I know, I know."

Another town, another darkened gas station. "Jane, what if I pulled over and you went into the woods and— "

"Mother! You always told me—"

"I know what I told you, but just this one time—"

"Mommy, find a bathroom, *please.*"

The road curves sharply around a bend as they enter another town. The car's headlights illuminate a town limit sign.

Bethlehem. Population 805.

Up ahead are the lights of a filling station and Mary exhales in relief. But as she rolls up to the pumps she sees that it too is closed. She looks up and down the street. Store windows are dark. There is no traffic. Everything in Bethlehem has closed for Christmas Eve.

Then, Mary realizes there is only one place likely to be open for business on this particular night, and that's when she sees it across the street, the steeple and the back of a small church, with a floodlit manger scene in front, and she amuses herself with the thought that if there is no place for them in the inn, then they must make other arrangements. "Come with me, Jane," she says. "You too, Dick."

They cross the street and walk through the church parking lot, where there is an oddity: a sleigh, parked at the edge, no reindeer. Mary sees a door on the side of the church. All of Bethlehem is silent as they step across a lawn growing white with snow. Mary turns the knob and the door opens.

At once they collide with a wall of sound.

They are standing in the side aisle of a full sanctuary in joyous celebration. It is *packed*! Pews are crowded with people standing shoulder-to-shoulder holding hymnals and singing in full-throated splendor. It is a symphony of voices and organ music. Dozens of heads turn toward the unexpected visitors in the doorway. Mary smiles in embarrassment. Her children stand in shock, and hurriedly she pushes them against their skidding shoes to the back of the church and a small narthex.

She is handed a bulletin by an usher and without thinking she takes it. She asks about restrooms. Downstairs.

"Dick, wait here," she says and then grabs Jane's hand. The wood steps creak as they descend a narrow set of stairs, which turn sharply before ending at the edge of a spacious fellowship hall.

There, they are surprised to find Santa Claus, bearded, booted, and buttoned, pulling on a red cap and admiring himself in a mirror.

"Excuse me," Mary apologizes, and Santa replies with a booming *ho-ho-ho.* Jane's eyes shine like big blue ornaments. Mary pulls her to the women's room and tells her to go in, saying, "I'll wait for you upstairs."

Upstairs, Dick is gone. He is not in the narthex.

Mary asks the usher, who answers, "I think he stepped outside, ma'am."

Mary goes out the front door and stands on the steps and peers into the snowfall and notices the nativity scene on the church's side lawn. Up close, she sees that the figures are not painted plywood cutouts but real people and animals, a live nativity. The players are dressed in robes and head covers, all except one, who is wearing a down jacket and stocking cap. It is Dick.

Mary hurries to his side. She notices he is holding one end of a rope secured to the neck of a goat. He is staring at the manger and doesn't see his mother until she is next to him. He smiles broadly.

"Mom, isn't this great?" he whispers. "They needed another shepherd, so they picked me."

Mary stands there for several minutes, pleased that Dick is enjoying himself. But then she looks at her watch and whispers in his ear, "Dick, we have to go."

"Just a little while longer," he answers. "The wise men haven't given their gifts yet. And they need an angel. Do you want to be an angel?"

"I'll be back. I have to get your sister." Mary goes back inside.

The women's room is empty. Santa is stuffing wrapped gifts into an oversized sack when he says to Mary, "She went upstairs right after you left."

But the narthex is empty. Not even the usher is there. Mary peers through a side window into the sanctuary, which is dark, lights off. Slowly, she opens the door and hears hundreds of voices singing *Silent Night.*

All is calm, all is bright

Everyone is holding a candle, including Jane, standing behind the last pew. The tiny flame shines on her face like a light from within. She hands her mother a bulletin and an unlit candle.

"This one's for you, Mommy. Watch. I learned how to do it".

She instructs her mother how to hold her candle as it is being lit and together they sing the last two verses.

The service ends and they go outside to the manger scene, which now has a larger audience. But Dick is gone. Mary looks everywhere for him, including the car, and then returns to the church.

She follows the sound of voices downstairs to the fellowship hall, where grown-ups are watching their children form a line in front of Santa Claus. Dick is in line, and has saved a place for his sister. Mary accepts a cup of coffee from the man she recognizes as the usher, and as each child advances toward Santa they receive a gift-wrapped present from the big sack at his feet. Finally, all the children are taken care of and Santa stands, puts the sack on his shoulder, waves good-bye, and punctuates his departure with his best *ho-ho-ho* of the night. Dick and Jane each get a cookie and Mary thanks everyone she passes as she leads her children up the stairs to the exit.

As she starts the car, her phone rings in her purse. It's her husband Jeff.

"I was expecting you an hour ago," he says. "Where *are* you?"

"Bethlehem, where else would we be tonight?" She laughs.

When Jeff is slow to answer, she says, "We had a wonderful time. I'll tell you everything when I get home."

On her way out of town Mary drives in front of the church and notices the sleigh is gone. Its runners have etched parallel tracks in the snow that disappear into the night.

"We told Santa where we live," Dick says, "in case he thought we lived here."

Jane reclines in her seat and just before she drifts off to sleep she says to her mother, "I'm glad we didn't find a gas station."

What if there had been room in the inn?

What if a dozen fewer people had showed up for the census and there had been a vacancy and Mary and Joseph didn't have to settle for the manger? The story would have been the same, but it also would have been different. The star in the east would still have been a signal pointing to the birth of the Christ child, but a warm bed would have replaced straw bales, and the revelry of guests down the hall celebrating their night in the city would have disturbed the peace, and, befitting of a modern Christmas, the wise men might have picked up their myrrh in the inn's gift shop. No, this king had to enter the world in a humble place to match the humility of the lessons he was saving for us. If there had been room in the inn, the story would have been wrong. The lyrics of time-honored carols wouldn't be the same. Live nativity scenes would have to be designed differently and include a landlord. And the worst part of all: after getting a tip from the angels and walking a long way in a dust cloud trailing their flocks to attend Christ's birth, the shepherds would have been told to stay outside.

Merry Christmas.

A Christmas Carol

2013

(Charles Dickens' Christmas Carol is a classic story about the redeeming grace of Christmas. This is a more contemporary story about Christmas's redeeming grace)

Doug came home from college to start his Christmas break on the same day of a family tradition: a night of house-to-house caroling in the neighborhood. Every year his mother and father were the organizers of the event. When Doug entered the house they were sitting at the kitchen table arranging the hymns they would sing, setting aside copies of the music for the aunts and uncles and cousins who would be joining them later.

"Who'd you get a ride with?" his father asked Doug.

"Tommy," Doug answered, opening the refrigerator door. "I asked him if he wanted to join us and he said maybe later. He missed his girlfriend."

"And you didn't?" his mother asked.

"Of course I did." He reached over and gave her a hug. "But now I'm home."

"Smooth," his father said.

The carolers assembled after dinner. They stood on the sidewalk and greeted each other in their winter coats and scarves and stocking caps. They admired the galaxy of Christmas lights lining both sides of Sycamore Street. Doug's father delivered his customary pre-carol pep talk. "Remember what we're doing tonight," he said. "We're taking a solemn oath to bring the good news. Tonight, we are the Lord's angels announcing Christ's birth."

Doug's mother humored her husband. "Okay," she said to the group, "everyone follow Gabriel."

They would sing to every house on the block. Down one side and then the other. A dozen hymns for a dozen houses. Two hours at the most, including time to accept the invitations of a few neighbors to come inside for refreshments and the chance to warm up, which for the adults meant their insides, too. At most houses, porch lights would come on and neighbors would step outside for a few chilly minutes to enjoy their personal carol and then thank the singers with shouts of Merry Christmas.

The carolers sang "O Come All Ye Faithful" to the Spencers and "Hark the Herald Angels Sing" to the Schmidts, who offered the singers hot chocolate and cookies before sending them on their way again. They crossed the street and sang to the Taylors, "On Jordan's Bank the Baptist's Cry", a favorite of Doug's mother.

Not all the neighbors were welcoming. Take, for example, Mr. Brophy, the sixth neighbor on the route. Every year he stayed inside while the carolers sang in front of his house. He was always home, a light shone in his living room, but he wouldn't come to the door. He never had.

For years, Frank Brophy had been at odds with his neighbors. He was friendly enough while in his driveway, waving to passers-by who knew him, but he refused invitations to their parties and other gatherings, usually without an RSVP. *Keeps to himself* was an apt description of him. Nobody knew much about him, other than he was a widower living alone.

There were rumors he was a drinker, but only rumors.

What was known for certain was that he complained about everything, about parked cars in front of his yard, loose dogs, creeping crabgrass, and noise after dark. Things were worse for the kids in the neighborhood. Frank Brophy had no tolerance for kids riding their bikes in his driveway or running across his lawn or playing in the street. Over the years, by Doug's count, Mr. Brophy had seized a half dozen footballs that bounced errantly into his front yard, a kite that crashed-landed on his roof, and Tommy Harrell's remote-controlled race car that veered off course for an unplanned pit stop in Brophy's open garage. The boys on Sycamore Street retaliated with acts of vandalism, using weapons like soap, toilet paper, and raw eggs. They scribbled threatening messages on his sidewalk, and discovered that while chalk disappears in the rain, spray paint does not. That happened one year when they were particularly nasty. Doug's father made them scrub the concrete clean again.

The carolers moved to the front of Brophy's darkened porch and sang "Silent Night". When they were done Doug's father commented that it was a waste of Christmas's best hymn, and then stomped off to the next house. After a pause to see if Brophy would make a surprise appearance on his porch, the caroling crew followed. Doug held back for another moment, his thoughts awash with the memories of long-ago battles with Frank Brophy.

And a secret he had been keeping for some time, about his last crime against Brophy. It happened five years ago.

Behind Brophy's house was a new cul-de-sac with houses that had been built after Doug went away to college. Before that, it was a vacant lot that made the best baseball field for blocks around. The size and shape of the lot were perfect for a ball park, with the wood fence across Brophy's backyard—referred to by the Sycamore Street boys as the *Brown Monster*—serving as a left field wall off which many doubles and triples had caromed, but too far from home plate for anyone to clear with a home run, or so the boys had thought for a long time.

It was Doug who made sandlot history.

In the last game to be played on the sandlot, he tagged one of Charlie Spencer's hanging curves and smashed a deep fly ball toward the fence. All eyes were on the ball's arcing flight as leftfielder Tommy Harrell raced back until he ran out of room and stopped to watch the ball sail thirty feet over his head and the fence.

Touch them all, Doug's teammates hollered.

Doug waved his arms and was about to start his home run trot when they all heard it: a loud crash and the unmistakable sound of broken glass sprinkling on wood, presumably Brophy's backyard deck.

Doug didn't touch them all. He didn't touch a single base. The boys grabbed their bats and gloves and scattered like mice. Within seconds, the lot was empty, with no clues of the game left behind. It was the last baseball game ever played on the vacant lot. After that, the boys of Sycamore Street walked a mile to the high school to play ball. They vowed to never utter a word about what had happened. If it was discussed at all, usually in a whisper, the incident was referred to as the *unsolved crime*.

Doug ran to catch up with the carolers.

Next, they sang "We Three Kings Of Orient Are" to the Fitzpatricks, and then went inside for hot cider and Tom and Jerrys. There were three houses left on the block, when Doug suddenly discovered he had dropped a glove somewhere and told the others not to wait for him as he retreated to find it. With a flashlight he retraced his steps on the sidewalk. In front of Brophy's house, with his eyes and flashlight beam directed downward, he heard a voice.

"Was it the left hand?"

Startled, Doug looked up to see a shadowed figure on Brophy's front porch.

"What?"

"I asked if it was a left hand. The glove you're looking for."

It was Frank Brophy.

"Yeah. I dropped it somewhere."

Brophy raised his arm. "I got it right here."

Doug froze, uncertain what to do next. In his mind he saw his entire childhood as misdirected flights of footballs, baseballs, and kites: the only things that up to this moment had connected the lives of the two of them. Now a glove. The boys of Sycamore Street used to speculate what Brophy did with all the stuff he took. Did he throw everything out with the trash? Did he build a shrine in a spare bedroom to showcase the spoils of wars with the boys?

Cautiously, Doug approached the house. He was about to say thanks when Frank Brophy asked, "So, how do you like college?"

Stunned by the question, Doug hesitated before answering. "Fine. It's good."

"Glad to hear it. You're in your third year, right?"

"Yeah…. third year."

"Say, I've got something for you. Why don't you come inside for a minute?"

Doug stopped breathing. He had never set foot inside the House of Brophy. In their youth, besides the talk of a shrine of stolen kid stuff, he and his friends imagined rooms decorated like scenes from stories crafted by Edgar Allan Poe, tributes to horror, maybe a tell-tale heart beating beneath a floor, or a pit and a pendulum in a dark basement, or a raven in a cage. Kids believed in those things.

But Doug felt he had no choice but to accept Brophy's invitation and step inside.

The house was warm and the living room was small and tidy, crowded by a card table around which three middle-aged men sat. On the table were knives and pieces of plastic, brushes, and tubes of paint and glue.

The men looked up, and one of them asked, "Who's your friend, Frank?"

"This is Doug. He lives across the street. He's one of the carolers."

"Well, then," a second man said," I have to ask you, Frank. What kind of friend are you if you don't get up to go outside and listen to him sing?"

"I could hear them okay," Brophy replied. "Silent Night. Maybe next Christmas we'll *all* go outside and listen."

"Frank, Frank, Frank.." the man continued, "every year it's the same excuse. What do we have to do? *Push* you out the door?"

"Anyway," Brophy said, "I invited Doug to come in because I have a gift for him."

"Doug, take off your coat and stay awhile," the third man said. "There's egg nog in the kitchen and we could use a hand."

"What are you guys doing?" Doug asked.

"Making Christmas ornaments. We give them to the homeless shelter and orphanage."

"Doug has lived across the street his whole life," Brophy said. "Now he's in college. Studying to be an engineer."

"Is that so? Well, Doug, how about doing some engineering for us? We're pretty good with our hands but weak at design. We're making too many stars and angels. Got any ideas?"

"I don't know," Doug answered, shrugging. "Maybe people in a homeless shelter would like an ornament that's a house, like the one they hope to have someday. Can you make little houses, maybe houses decorated for Christmas?"

"We can make *anything*," was the reply. "Ralph, why don't you turn your inn into a rambler? Put a wreath on it. Nobody's going to guess it's supposed to be an inn."

"Why don't you stay and help us?" Brophy asked, handing a paper bag to Doug.

"Thanks, but I should get back and join the others. And thanks for finding my glove." He held up the bag. "And the gift."

"Well, you're welcome to come back after the caroling is done," Brophy said. "We've got a long night ahead of us."

They exchanged goodbyes and Doug went outside. He ran to catch up with the carolers in front of the last house, the Hartman's, next door to Doug's. They sang, "Joy to the World" and called it a night.

Back home, Doug sat at the kitchen table and opened the bag and peered inside.

"What is it, Doug?" his mother asked. "What did Frank give you?"

Doug reached in and pulled out an odd-looking piece, a cylinder with glass on its sides, and....*what was it?*

It was a Christmas tree ornament. Handmade. It was a glass cylinder with tiny garlands and ribbons glued all around the outside. And mounted inside....a baseball. But it wasn't a new one. It was bruised and some of its stitches were frayed and loose.

Doug held it up and turned it. He stared at the baseball inside the glass. And something else.

He remembered. The memory he had pondered earlier in the evening, the one about the last baseball game, did an encore, but this time in his conscience.

"Frank Brophy made that?" his mother asked. "Well, isn't that something. Where do you suppose he got the idea? Here, let me see it." In slow motion, Doug handed it to her.

"My, that's wonderful," his mother said, spinning the ornament. Her husband looked over her shoulder.

"Well, look at that," he said. "The glass is cracked. That's too bad. You didn't drop it, did you, Doug?"

Doug didn't hear his father. He stared at the ornament with glazed eyes.

"Doug?" his father repeated. "What's the matter?"

A smile crept across Doug's face, small at first, growing until it hung ear to ear. He thought about calling Tommy Harrell. "Nothing," he said. "It's okay."

"What a nice gift," said his mother. She got up and went to the living room and hung the ornament on the tree. His father put his arm on his wife's shoulder and said, "I guess Frank knew how much Doug likes baseball." Together, they admired the gift. "Doug," he asked, "are you sure you didn't drop it?"

They heard the front door slam.

"Doug?"

"Where did he go?"

Doug stood on his front step and looked across the street. On Frank Brophy's front porch, the light had been turned on.

Indestructible

2014

L et's celebrate children's Christmas programs everywhere. We can't say enough about them. And let's hear it for the program directors who make them happen.

Let's hear it for the children, too. They enrich the greatest story ever told in ways only children can do. They don't know it but as they move about the stage struggling with their lines they are teaching us something as great as the story itself. They prove that the Christmas Story is indestructible.

Nothing can ruin the Christmas Story. Every year we put it in the tiny hands of children with the chore of reminding us again how great it is. Perfect children perform imperfectly but the story retains its greatness. The missed lines and wandering stage directions and falling props will alter the story's path but cannot undo its majesty. Cardboard mangers get knocked down and costumes slip and shepherds poke angels with their crooks and the story goes on. The plot flies off in new and unexpected directions but we know where it will land.

Only children can do this. They play their parts with a pure innocence and press on in the midst of accidents and surprises only the audience notices. They show no embarrassment. They act as if the gaffes are part of the story. And in a way they are; the original Christmas story included surprise, disappointment, and improvisation. And innocence.

All Christmas program directors will say something like this:

"No matter what happens every year, the main story line never loses its direction. It's like a train that comes off its rails but reaches the station anyway. I'm confident that if the entire set collapsed and all the children stood around petrified in fear, the program would still move forward to its successful ending. An angel would reach down to touch one or two of the children and magically they would step up and save the show with an unrehearsed miracle, doing whatever feels natural. For a good Christmas program, the prepared script is only a starting place."

"If everything went off without a hitch, well.. how boring would that be? The original Christmas was unscripted. The manger was a last-minute choice. "

At every church you will find the world's *greatest* Christmas Program Director. They are everywhere. Their identities are no secret. All CPD's are the greatest. They deserve our applause and the chance to take a mighty bow. They are the parents and teachers and Christian education directors and pastors who work hard to produce programs to be perfect when they know they probably won't be.

They give every child a part. There is never a shortage of parts. If an extra kid shows up unexpectedly, another angel or sheep is added to the cast. The angels are the cutest, played by the youngest. They *show up* as angels and slip into their roles convincingly. The older children are given reading parts and show their pride in successful recitations with smiles so big their small faces can't hold them.

And then there is Mary, who must act divine and purposeful. The audience never takes its eyes off Mary, and, thus, she has the most important part. She carries the greatest responsibility, particularly if the baby Jesus in her arms is real—rather than a doll—and has been temporarily adopted from the *real* mother seated nervously on the edge of her seat in the front pew.

All of the world's greatest CPD's have their own stories to tell. Their stories begin with, "There was a child in one of my programs I'll never forget."

Here's one. It's about a boy, Kevin.

"Kevin was shy and rarely spoke," the director says, "but I knew he was creative. Once, in Sunday School, the children were drawing pictures of Bible stories and Kevin drew an airplane. I asked what story he was drawing and he answered the flight from Egypt. I didn't know how to respond.

But then *he* got in the last word. He pointed to the face he had drawn in the airplane's window and said, 'He's the pilot. He's Pontius'.

It was okay for him to mix Bible stories. At least he was learning.

For the Christmas program every year Kevin never volunteered for a speaking part, which was surprising because he was careful enough and would have handled a speaking part better than most of the other children. Every year he chose to be a shepherd and preferred to stand quietly in the back. So, while other less-able children wandered around the stage forgetting their lines or singing loudly off-key, Kevin stood quietly.

Something remarkable happened in Kevin's last program. For the first time ever it appeared the program would be flawless. The props stayed up and the children took their places on cue and nobody missed a line. Oh, there were a couple surprises, like when one of the angels left his spot on stage to tickle baby Jesus and one little girl lifted up her robe to study its hem. And one of the wise men announced his gift as *frankenstein*. But nothing big.

That year we built an inn on the stage and decorated it with big block letters spelling *Bethlehem* above the door. The letters were *huge*. The program was nearing its end and the children were positioning themselves to take their final bows when suddenly the innkeeper stumbled while coming through the door and bumped against the wall of the inn. The wall waved and the letters shook. The "L" rattled loose and crashed to the floor, fortunately not striking anyone, and rolled over until it landed flat at the edge of the stage.

The audience fell silent. Parents lowered their camcorders. The children turned around to read they were now in *Beth-e-hem*.

No one uttered a sound, until Kevin finally spoke, raising the program to its proper place of indestructibility."

"It's a *Noel* Christmas, everyone!"

'Tis The Season

2015

I don't have to tell you what season this is. It's Advent. But you'd be surprised how many church pastors at one time or another have heard someone in their congregation say, "We should sing more Christmas songs in December. They sound so *nice*, and it's the season"—to which the pastor has replied with a question, "Which season is that?"

We know it's not the Christmas season *yet*. We can only shake our heads at the confusion created by others. Out *there*, in the tinseled world of *Happy Holidays*, the merchants and sorcerers of commercialism are trying to convince us the Christmas season has already begun. But we know better. Despite all the holiday cheer, it's not Christmas. Today is the 3rd Sunday of Advent.

We also know the *difference* between Christmas and Advent. One is the special event that is Christ's birth and the other is how we get ready for it. We see them as interlaced, but with different messages. But to the unenlightened who have fallen victim to the sorcerer's spell, all the clamor and haste this time of year is Christmas, one big, colorful celebration that starts with a buying frenzy on Black Friday and ends when the last gift is opened. From this viewpoint, Christmas the day is hard to distinguish from Christmas the event. The *Twelve Days of Christmas* is just the title of a silly song. The sacred becomes secular.

Advent may be something the sorcerers can't sell, and that's fine with me. Like you, I find joy in Happy Holiday traditions, but when we keep Advent *away* from Happy Holidays, it retains its own special identity. It stands alone under a bright light of clarity, free from all the other stuff that distracts and deafens us at Christmas. In some ways it is better than Christmas, which is the thesis I want to prove. We should celebrate Advent as much, if not more, as we celebrate Christmas.

I have five points on which to make this case.

First, it's liturgically correct. As you know, Christmas won't begin until December 25th. In the meantime, we prepare. Advent is more about us than the Christ child. Christ's birth was foretold by prophets, and it is our duty to ponder this prophecy and ask, "are we ready for what's to come?" We've received some *big* news. What will we do to straighten the path and fill the valleys ahead? You may know that the word *advent* was derived from Latin, *adventus* means coming. Advent celebrates the *coming* of Christ more than Christmas does.

Two, how appropriate it is that Advent occurs when the days are their shortest. This time of year daylight is scarce and darkness surrounds us. Advent is the time before the light arrives. As we shop and decorate and party and bake our way toward Christmas, a galaxy of artificial lights encircles and blinds us, but still some of the dark peeks through. We squint into the glare and ask, "Is *this* what it's all about?" Then, we look the other way, and the tiny flames of four Advent candles, lit one at a time, draw our attention and we never see the darkness again.

Three, there are beautiful but haunting minor chords in the standard bearer of Advent hymns, "O Come, O Come Emmanuel." Yes, it is *not* a Christmas song, it is an Advent hymn. The melody is slightly unsettling, but the words comfort and remind us to remain cheerful. They foretell the coming light. Listen.

"*O come thou dayspring bright, pour on our souls thy healing light, dispense the long night's lingering gloom, and pierce the shadows of the tomb.*" This is what it's all about. *This* isn't tinsel and reindeer. If the sorcerers were to say, "That's not a Christmas song," they'd be right for a change.

Four, waiting for something good to happen can be *good* for you. Hope and anticipation, mixed with delayed gratification, are healthy. It must be a Christian thing that the rest of the world can't grasp but we do the same thing at Easter. We celebrate the good news of the resurrection *on* Easter, and not before, but we also celebrate Lent, the time preceding the big day, as a time for reflection and preparation. We wait weeks before getting to the end of the story. So it is with the Christmas story. We don't rush the part about Jesus' birth.

And five, last but not least, the greatest meaning can come from the smallest acts. We celebrate Advent with the minimum of ornaments. What could be so simple as a wreath on which we arrange four candles and some greenery, light one candle, and then wait a whole week before we light the next one? Or, how about what an Advent calendar can teach our kids? It's a family thing, every day during the season, one door at a time. Not all at once. Every door is a chapter of the story and the chapters are as important as how the story will end. Slow down and enjoy them. *He* is coming. *This* season is special.

Away In The Manger—Part 1

2016

David walked down the length of the train until he found an open boxcar door. He tossed his rucksack inside and pulled himself up. He was not surprised to discover the car was already occupied. Many homeless men were hopping freights to get around, and three other men were inside the car huddled around a coffee pot over a small stove. They looked up at David with no visible alarm or fear.

"Aren't you afraid of settin' the floor on fire?" David asked.

"Not if you do it right," one of the men answered. He was the one tending the stove, while the other two curled their hands around steaming cups. David saw that all were older than he.

"Where you gents headed?" David asked.

"Littleton," the second one answered. "And you?"

"Bethlehem. Know where it is?"

"Of course. Don't you?"

"Yeah. I was just askin' if you knew."

"I used to know a fella' from Bethlehem. He was a carpenter," one of the cup-holders said. "I don't know where he ended up though."

"Are you going there for the census?" the third one asked David.

"Yeah," David answered with noticeable exasperation.

"Sorry to hear that."

David took a seat against one of the walls and undid the straps on his pack. He set out his water bottle and cup and food bag. There was one ham sandwich left. He unfolded the wax paper and after smelling the meat took a bite.

The one with his back facing David got up and walked over holding the pot by its handle. "Coffee?"" he asked, and David held up his cup.

"Thanks. Say, you boys know anything about the yards between here and Bethlehem?"

"If you're wondering about bulls, this yard is the one to worry about. Once we get out of here we'll be okay."

"If we haven't been spotted yet," said another, "we should be fine. The bulls check trains comin' in, not goin' out."

And then, as if queued to the man's remark, there was a series of banging sounds and the train lurched and began to creep forward. The springs creaked and the wheels squealed under the floor. The four of them stayed in the shadows away from the door as the train gained speed and began to clear the yard. The view through the door changed from empty lots with fences and barrels and stacks of pallets to a thick forest and an occasional pasture. David moved to the door while the others remained in the corner drinking their coffee and smoking hand-mades. The first man turned off the stove and reached into his bag and took something out. It was a checkerboard, and he set it up on the floor.

"So, where you coming from?" David was asked. "Someplace better than Bethlehem, I hope."

David laughed. "Oh, don't you boys recognize me? My face is on billboards everywhere. Name is Rockefeller. I was the lucky millionaire. I lost everything in the crash but still had the sense not to jump out of a window on Wall Street with all my friends." The others looked back at David with blank expressions. David went on in a quieter tone. "I worked in an automobile plant in Detroit. Got let go last month."

"Nobody named Rockefeller has to report for the census," said the first man.

"Morgenthau, maybe," said the second. And all three laughed.

David let it go. He knew what they were saying. Only Jewish families had to return to their hometowns for the census. And this was the first time for a census of Jews. The first *ever*. The previous president would never have put up with such a crime, but the nation had grown tired of his New Deal and voted him out of office after only one term. His treasury secretary had been Morgenthau, a Jew. The new president was different, sticking to his election promise of the keeping the country out of war and rounding up all the Jews at home. By the end of the year Jews had to report to their hometowns to be counted and taxed. There were rumors about what might happen after that, and none of them were good. Folks had started calling the new president the *German*. After all, that's what he was.

David sat by the door drinking his coffee and watching the changing landscape. The train entered the mountains and ascended into clouds. Snowflakes swirled in the gray air, light at first, and then grew into a storm.

There was already a white dusting on the ground. He guessed it was mid-afternoon. He turned the collar up on his coat.

"King me," said the second man.

The train climbed a grade in a series of turns and leveled off and passed a depot that read Crawford Station. The sky cleared and the sun came out to shine on David's face. The train didn't stop at the depot, which was for passenger trains and the people who could afford to buy a ticket on one. It wouldn't stop in Bethlehem either, but would slow down enough for David to jump.

An hour later he pulled on his rucksack and got ready.

"I guess I forgot to ask," he said. "What's in Littleton?"

"It's kind of hard to explain," said the third man, the one not playing checkers.

"You boys aren't running from the law, are you?"

"Nothing like that. Are you?"

Before David could answer, the second man said, "We're on kind of a treasure hunt."

"Can I ask you something?" the third man asked.

"Suit yourself."

"Do you believe in prophecies?"

"What?"

"Prophecies. Do you believe in signs of the future?"

David shifted his eyes from one man to another, unsure where the odd question was headed. But he guessed it had to do with Littleton.

"Yeah, I suppose I do. But I don't know if I've ever seen one."

"How would you know if you haven't?"

A long silence followed.

"Crown me, too," said the first man. "This game ain't over yet."

"What'll you do after the census?" asked the third man. "They're not makin' cars in Bethlehem."

"Something will come up." He shrugged. "I'll stick around for the New Year." He looked in the third man's eyes with all the hope he could muster, but he knew it wasn't much.

The man's return look was sympathetic. Sympathy was probably all he had to give. There was a lot of it going around these days.

"At any rate, you boys take it easy," David said. And then he leapt from the boxcar and landed hard on the gravel beside the tracks. He rolled and sprang to his feet and looked up to watch the train continue on its way. Littleton was the next town. The three men stood at the door of the car and waved good-bye.

The train curved out of sight and David was struck by a strange thought: that since leaving Detroit he had ridden several freights and met a lot of men looking for work, but not once had there been an exchange of names, and the notion that men in a common struggle would keep their identities to themselves saddened him. They shared their futures of uncertainty and despair, but not their names.

The sun began to set behind the mountains and David found his way in the twilight to the center of town. He took a piece of paper from his pocket and read directions to the Granite State Shelter, which, he was told, had once been a school. He remembered when he was a boy and there were no shelters. Now they were needed. There had been three schools and he wasn't sure which one was converted to a shelter. But he had an address. He hadn't been in Bethlehem for ten years and everybody he knew back then, friends and family, were gone. He recognized some businesses. Hammer's Drug. Manger's Garage. The Old Town Inn. He could rent a room at the Inn but he preferred to save his money and stay for free at the shelter.

He found it and went in the front door. At the welcome counter he waited in a line of men to claim a bed for the night. In a few minutes, it was his turn.

"Last one," the attendant behind the counter told David. "After you, we're full. We'll have to turn people away."

"Is it because of the census?" David asked.

The attendant gave him an incredulous look, as if David had offended him.

"What?" David asked.

"Where've you been? We're full *every* night. Census or homeless, evicted, in search of work—take your pick. We see them all. It's been like this for months."

"Sorry, I didn't know."

"It's okay. I'm supposed to ask you if you're here for the census but I didn't vote for the German so I figure it's none of my business. You look like an honest fellow." When David didn't reply, he continued, "There's hot soup in the dining room."

"Thanks."

Not wanting to pass on a free meal, David went straight to the soup line. The dining room was half-full, men alone or with families, sitting close together over soup and bread. No one looked up and there was only quiet conversation between people, with one exception, a card game at a table in the corner, where four men sat holding cards fanned out in their hands and fingering piles of coins in front of them.

David ate his soup while sitting near the card players. While he ate, he listened to them. They played poker.

He thought about tomorrow. The duties of the census would take little time. He should be done by mid-morning. To get a bed at the shelter for another night, he would need to return to claim one by noon. Then, he would go out again to look for work, any job he could find. Maybe one of the businesses in town was hiring. If nothing came up, he would go to Littleton. There could be opportunities there, or else why would the three men on the train be going there?

The poker players finished a hand with a flurry of noise and one of them got up and announced he was done. "That's enough for me," he said, sweeping a few coins from the table into a flattened palm with the edge of his other hand. "I'm turning in early."

After he left, one of the remaining players turned to David and asked, "Interested in sittin' in? Five card stud."

David shrugged. He had some pocket money. "Sure." He changed tables. There were no introductions. He had a buck-and-a-half in coins but only put a dollar's worth on the table. He buried the remaining fifty cents in his back pocket. Tomorrow's lunch money. His budget could afford to lose no more than a buck. Better not be tempted to play with any more than he could afford to lose.

He began with a lucky streak, winning three of the first five hands and tripling his stake. Then, his luck turned and he lost the next four. One time he folded even though he held a pair of sevens after four cards, both face down, such was the certainty his luck was not about to turn.

The dining room cleared out and only the poker players were left. Once in a while someone entered the shelter and David could see them in the entry asking for a bed, only to be turned away. There was even a couple, the woman pregnant.

David felt he was due for some good luck. He won a small pot and then was dealt the hand he was certain would put him ahead for the night.

After four cards—one facedown and three face-up—David was holding two pair, queens and sevens. Only the pair of sevens and one queen was showing. The other queen was hidden. The man to his right was showing two jacks. When the man confidently bet a dollar, only David matched him. The other two fellows folded.

Then the last card was dealt facedown.

David drew a third queen. Full house. He struggled to look calm.

The other man, showing a pair of jacks, noticed that David had only two quarters left and bet another dollar to scare him off. David thought about the coins in his back pocket, tomorrow's lunch money, but chose to stay with his original plan. He felt he wouldn't lose the hand, not with a full house, but he would stick with the plan. There was almost four dollars in the pot, the biggest of the night.

"Is my credit good?" he asked. When nobody said anything, he got his answer that it was not.

"Well, as you can see," he continued, "I can't cover your bet. But what will you take instead? What's my bed tonight worth to you? Fifty cents?"

The man with jacks eyed him curiously. "What's an extra bed do for me?"

"You've seen all the people coming in here. You can sell it. I bet it's worth more than fifty cents."

By the surprised look on the man's face, David could tell the man hadn't thought of that.

He nodded.

David tossed in his last two quarters and then smiled as he flipped over his two queens. He was about to reach for the pot when the man with jacks turned over his two hidden cards: two more jacks. Four jacks beat a full house. He raked the pile of coins from the center of the table to his side.

"I'll sell you your bed back," the man said, chuckling to himself. "but you're right. It's worth more than fifty cents. Supply and demand. Perhaps you've heard of it."

The players took their possessions and left the room without saying good-byes. Stunned, David sat at the table by himself for another minute. The room was suddenly silent as a tomb. The soup was gone. So was the bread. The legs of his chair scraped loudly as he rose to his feet. He slung his rucksack over his shoulder and walked through the entryway and out the front door and into the night.

Away In The Manger—Part 2

2017

D avid walked down Bethlehem's darkened Main Street. The street was empty, shops were closed, and lights were off. Only one car rolled by as he walked along the sidewalk. He cursed himself for gambling away his bed at the shelter. Now he faced a night out in the cold. At least he wasn't hungry.

He thought about what Bethlehem was like when he was growing up. He tried to remember places that might take him in tonight. But he recalled nothing. He didn't know anybody in Bethlehem anymore.

At the center of town, where Main Street crossed the river, he stopped on the bridge to look around. The river rushing underneath made a sighing sound and the rocks in its path were covered with a white icing.

Downstream, in the forest along the river bank, David saw that there was a campfire. He could see a flickering flame and the shadows of men moving in front of it. He knew of such camps, places where men on the move gathered to spend the night together. They were safe places mostly. Sometimes there could be danger. David decided he could take the risk and he left the bridge and made his way through the trees toward the camp.

The camp was nothing more than a clearing in the woods next to the river and a fire pit in the middle of bare ground where two men had laid out their bedrolls. They sat on the ground close to the fire. One read a newspaper in the dim yellow light of the fire.

"Mind if I sit?" David asked.

Neither man answered. One nodded his head.

David took off his rucksack and kneeled by the fire on the opposite side from the other two. He warmed his hands close to the flame.

"I saw you at the shelter tonight," one of the men said. "You couldn't get a bed either?"

Rather than explain, David gave him a simple answer by just shaking his head. He glanced around the camp. There was evidence of its use. Empty cans were scattered at its edges. A couple items of clothing. And what appeared to be a blanket. David's bedroll was thin so he stood and went to the blanket and picked it up. He folded it under his arm and returned to the fire.

"Where you fellows from?" David asked. He noticed they were passing a bottle between them.

"Pennsylvania. Nazareth. And you?"

"I was born and raised here but moved away. My last home was Detroit."

"Why the homecoming?"

David smiled, barely, almost to himself. "I guess I never thought of it that way." After a pause, he answered. "Census." He left it at that. The census was a political issue. Some people sided with the German and thought it was good for the country. Not David. But maybe these two fellows did. Why stir up an argument?

One of the men produced a crumpled paper bag. "You hungry?" he asked. "I've got some bread to go with the wine."

The other man held the bottle out for David. David wasn't a drinker but he regarded the invitation as something other than just drinking, something more important. He broke off a piece of bread and took a swig from the bottle. It tasted good. But more than that, just as he had felt bonds with other men he had met on the road the past couple days, he felt welcomed by these two. By accepting their gift, David was showing he trusted them.

They had been sitting by the fire for almost an hour and the light was beginning to dim when they heard a rustling sound in the nearby trees. Someone was approaching. David stiffened in fear. He peered hard in the direction of the sound until he saw three men emerging from the woods, and he recognized them as the men from the train, the men headed to Littleton.

"I hope we're not disturbing you fellows," one of them said.

"Not at all," was the reply. "Come and sit."

"Hey, look. It's our traveling companion," said another newcomer. "Rockefeller."

"Rockefeller?"

"It's an inside joke," David said to the men by the fire.

"Actually, we're just passing through." Looking at David, he said, "We got off the train before Littleton. We decided that's not where we want to go. We saw your fire and decided to stop and say hello."

The third newcomer peered up at the sky and pointed. "There it is," he said. All eyes looked up. David stood to get a better view.

Through the bare tree branches he saw a bright star, or a planet maybe. It hung low in the sky, the only heavenly body visible in that direction.

"My, but that star is bright," said the man holding the wine bottle.

"It's a planet," David answered. "Venus probably."

"Not to dispute your knowledge of astronomy," said the one who had pointed, "but that's east. Venus is...." He turned around and pointed the other way. "Venus is over there."

"I've never seen such a bright star," David said. "You know the name of it?"

When nobody answered, David looked at the three men standing. Even in the dim fire light he could read their expressions as they looked at each other. Their eyes were wide. They half-smiled as if sharing a secret.

"Star in the east?" one of them said, and all three laughed. Then, silence.

"We should be going," another one said finally. He looked at David and the two seated by the fire. "You gents are welcome to come with us."

"Where to?"

He nodded toward the east. "Wherever that star leads us."

"Do you fellows believe in prophecies?" another one standing asked.

"Sure. I guess," said one of the men on the ground.

"Well..."

This time the silence between them was awkward. Finally, one of the men standing said to his partner, "Tom, you can tell them. I can see these fellows aren't fascists." The use of that word, so political in the context of recent events, was disturbing and didn't seem to belong in the conversation they had enjoyed up until now. David trembled a little.

"I had a dream..." Tom began. He struggled with words before finding the course of what he wanted to say.

"I had a dream....it was the most real dream I've ever had. You have to believe me when I say that. There was an angel. And she spoke to me." He looked at David and the men seated on the ground squarely. "Don't ask me why the angel was a woman. She just *was*."

He continued. "I don't remember where I was in the dream, just that the angel came down out of the sky to tell me something important would happen *tonight*. And I was told where to go and what to look for. A star in the east, brighter than any star I've ever seen, would guide my way. I remembered everything after I woke up. Isn't that something? Most of the time I forget my dreams like that." He snapped his fingers.

David said nothing. The men seated on the ground were silent, too. Most likely they were thinking the same as David, that hard times will make you follow your hopes and dreams no matter how desperate they sound. Your mind can fill with strange thoughts. Your imagination can buck and leap.

Then, one of the other men from the train added, "I had the *exact* same dream."

"Me, too." said the 3rd.

The man who told the story about the dream nodded toward the eastern sky. "And there it is. Just like the angel said."

"What's supposed to happen?" David asked.

"The angel called him a king."

"Called who a king?"

"Whoever we're to meet there. Wherever the star takes us."

"A *king*?" said one of the men on the ground. "There are no kings anymore."

"You can believe that if you want. But king or no king, whoever it is, I believe it's somebody who was sent to us to help beat the German."

"*What* are you talkin' about? You talkin' about war?" asked one of the men on the ground.

"That's for the king to decide. But I don't think so."

"I dunno," said the other man on the ground, looking at his partner. "This sounds pretty strange to me."

"You don't have to go with us if you don't want to."

"Oh, I'd like to go with you. But how do you know it's not a trap? This could be a trap set by the German's people."

The three men standing seemed to have an answer to the question about the possibility of a trap but were hesitant to answer. Once again, they exchanged glances. David thought the man on the ground had a good point and needed a good reason to go with the three men.

Finally, one of them nodded his head toward Tom and Tom answered.

"The German can't get into my dreams, that's why."

"It's called faith," said the second.

"Just as it takes faith to share our dream with you fellows," said the third.

The conversation was over. Nobody spoke again. The three men from the train slowly walked away from the fire and disappeared into the dark. *Faith*, David thought. He had lost his when he lost his job, when the German took over, and when the census was ordered. He ached to feel faith again. Without speaking, David arose and, surprisingly, so did the other two. They got up and grabbed their stuff and kicked the fire out until it was just embers smoking in the dark. Then, the three of them hurried to catch up with the men from the train.

When he reached them, David asked, "How will you know we're at the place the star is pointing?"

But nobody answered. They stayed together, the six of them, and walked out of the woods and up the street. Looking up at the star, David had the sense it was growing brighter. But not closer. It remained in the distance. But at the same time, he felt a peculiar attraction to it, like it was pulling him up the street. The feeling grew the farther he walked. Yes. There could be no doubt that he and other men were going in the right direction to meet the king—or somebody—who was the subject of the prophecy that had been shared that night.

They came to an auto mechanic's shop. Beat-up cars and trucks were parked outside. The sign on the wall read *Manger's Garage*. David remembered it from his years growing up in Bethlehem.

There were two overhead doors and both were closed so they tried a side door instead and it swung open. Inside the garage it was completely dark, or such was David's first impression before they stepped through the doorway and were inside, where it was warm. In a corner, on the other side of a hoist that held a sedan five feet above the floor, a lantern was hanging from a wall bracket and there were people gathered in the yellow light underneath. David and the others inched closer.

What they saw was two men standing with their backs to the big room. They appeared to be standing watch over something. In front of them, in the very corner of the room, a woman sat on a torn bench seat that had been pulled from an automobile, his legs curled underneath her. She was wrapped in a blanket and in her arms was another blanket bunched around a quilt and in the folds of the quilt was a baby she was feeding. The mother looked up to see David and the others as they stepped around the hoist, and then the two men standing watch turned to look also. The six who had come from the riverbank stopped. Those wearing hats took them off.

"Hello, Joe," said one of the men David had met on the train. "Remember me? Charlie Wilson. I used to live here."

"Hello, Charlie."

The other man standing watch wore overalls with *Manger* stitched to the front. One of the men in David's group spoke, the one who had offered David wine at the campfire.

He spoke to Joe, not Manger.

"Are you the king?"

When neither man replied, Tom stepped forward. "What my friend means is that we're here because we learned that a king is coming and that he was sent to save us. That's all we know. We don't mean to make demands of anybody or anything. All we know is what some of us learned from our dreams, and our dreams told us to come here tonight. Does this make any sense?"

David was uncomfortable. He was sure they had come to the wrong place. They didn't belong here. Something wasn't right. The talk of a king—and the sight of a woman and her baby in a place as dark and dusty as a garage—was suddenly upsetting to him. He thought they should leave and look someplace else. This couldn't be the place the star pointed to.

But he could never have imagined what happened next.

"Welcome," said Manger to Tom. And then he nodded to the others. "We've been expecting you." That's all he said.

Manger and Joe turned toward the woman, and she took her eyes off the baby to look up at them. For several seconds they fixed their gazes on each other. No words were exchanged. Then a calm smile grew over the woman's face. It was small and delicate and expressed a feeling that was not triumphant, but it was a knowing smile conveying contentment, a quiet peace, and it comforted David. He stared at the woman in wonder and was struck by a curious feeling. It was not just the smile, not just the easy upturn of her mouth or rise in her cheeks. He saw emotion in her *eyes*, too. It was like her whole face was a reflection of pure joy that came from deep within. *How does she do that?* Whatever plot or conspiracy—or magic—there was in the air, she was in on it, too. She was a new mother, that much was known for sure, and there could be no doubt she was feeling all the elation the birth of a child brings, but the emotion in her face told David that she was feeling something greater than joy for herself or her baby. David was astonished that a simple smile could do this. She was real. And she could be an angel, too. At once David believed such things were possible.

Without anyone issuing a command, Tom, Charlie and the third man from the train stepped forward together. They passed Manger and Joe and went to the woman and knelt. They opened their rucksacks and pulled things out and set them on the ground in front of the car seat. David read the woman's lips. "Thank you." They rose and turned and shook hands with Manger and Joe.

Joe spoke to everyone.

"I'm sorry we haven't anything to offer you to eat or drink. But we're glad you're here. And don't feel you have to go. Stay if you want."

David said to Tom, "I'm sorry…but I didn't bring a gift. But will she take this blanket I found tonight?"

Tom smiled and patted him on the shoulder. "Why don't you give it to her?" And he did, looking up at her as he placed it on the seat. The smile never left her face.

Manger approached David and put an arm on his shoulder.

"Is he the father?" David asked, nodding toward Joe.

Manger didn't answer the question, but said something else. "You can give the baby something he'll need," he said.

"It's a boy, then."

"Yes," Manger answered. He went on. "But I have to ask you something important. Do you know what is happening here tonight?"

"No, but I want to learn. Tell me. What can I give him that he needs?"

"He needs what every child needs. A chance. But you have to know he's been sent here by God to save us, from the German and others, and from ourselves. Now that he's here, he's destined for great things, but he'll need our help."

"God sent him? I don't understand."

"Do you know what the prophecy was?"

"I didn't have the dream. These men told me about it."

"I know. I didn't send for you. I sent for them. But still, I'm glad you're here."

David's brow wrinkled. "Sent for them? What are you saying?"

"I'll tell you what the prophecy was. The German speaks like he follows God but really he is an enemy of all true believers. He has the power to do great harm and stop the world unless someone rises to oppose him and all others like him. He intends to use violence against all good people but we will use a stronger weapon. The truth. The baby will grow to become our savior. We have a lot to learn from him. You'll see. Call him a king if you like. King or not, he was sent from God. The world is about to turn again."

Manger continued.

"That's the prophecy. And you wouldn't be here if you didn't believe it, too. You may not have had the dream but the prophecy is for you also. I'm afraid we aren't the only ones who know about it. There are others, good and bad. Some are with the German. They know the baby is a threat to them. The German has given them orders to come here. And it is up to us to make sure they don't find him."

"What do you want me to do?"

"The three men who brought gifts, they are wise men, and they know about a place where the mother and child will be safe. It's far from here. I have a car ready to take them there. But I have to stay here and wait for the German's people and if I'm here when they arrive I can stall them and steer them the wrong way and be sure the mother and child get away safely. Know what I'm saying?"

"You want me to drive?"

"Yes. If you do this, it will be your gift to the child."

"But...I have to ask...who is the mother...where did she come from? Was she chosen? What is the plan for her?"

"You can ask anything you like. All your questions have answers."

"Which are?"

"There will be plenty of time for answers."

"I get it. You mean we're going to be traveling a long ways. I'll be driving for a long time with them. Right?"

Manger shrugged and smiled.

"I *was* going to say you have the rest of your life," he replied.

David nodded approvingly. "Fine, then," he said. He looked one more time at the mother. Happily, she was showing her baby to the others.

"You tell her," David added, "that I'll be ready to go any time she is. We can leave whenever she wants."

"You're doing a fine thing. She won't be long. The German's people may be here soon."

"I'm a good driver."

"I know you are."

"I'm honored to be asked to serve him."

"Bless you."

The Greatest Christmas Story

2018

Sometimes we look up to the sky to be entertained. Or to be inspired. We marvel at celestial events like rainbows, northern lights, and shooting stars. At the edges of the day the rising or setting sun paints the sky in bright colors. And when the earth inserts itself between the sun and moon we watch in awe as our shadow moves across the lunar surface. These are just a few things we see without a telescope.

We might call these events *heavenly*, and for good reason. Ancient cultures would read divine messages in sightings like these.

Our fascination with the sky started when we were children. We learned that the stars were so far away their light took years to get here, and that we could connect them into the shapes of animals and other figures. At Christmas our parents told us to look up and find Santa's sleigh. They would point to a satellite and say, "Look. There he is. Right on time."

In Sunday School we learned there had been a star above Bethlehem to mark Jesus's birthplace. After that we never lost our interest in the night sky at Christmas. There is something about Christmas Eve that makes us want to look up in wonder. Maybe another guiding star will appear and send us a modern message that we need today, like God's promise of peace and joy despite all our other troubles.

There was a Christmas Eve fifty years ago, some of us may recall, when we spent the evening gazing at the sky to find peace and joy. Millions of us, all at once, were looking up. What happened that night was extraordinary.

It was called Apollo 8 and it was on a mission that came to be known as *Christmas at the Moon.*

To understand the importance of the event, you first have to know something about the year that was ending. 1968 had been a turbulent and tragic year, marked by assassinations, war, dissent, racial unrest, and political upheaval. Some called the year apocalyptic. Even the Olympics were smeared by controversy. A national despair hung over us. We needed a lift to our spirits and Apollo 8 was about to give it to us.

The country was eight years into the decade in which our president had pledged to put men on the moon, and time was running out. To beat the Russians, mission schedules were moved up and Apollo 8, a necessary first step for the moon landing that would occur the following summer, took off just a few days before Christmas. We cheered as its three-member crew—Borman, Lovell, and Anders—became the first humans to leave the earth's orbit and head off into space.

It took them three days to reach the moon, arriving on Christmas Eve. Using high-tech rocketry, precise instruments, and principals of physics few of us understood, they steered the spacecraft from a straight-line direction to an orbital path around the moon. An on-board camera captured and beamed back to televisions on earth the closest images of the moon's surface we had ever seen. We saw what the astronauts saw: a barren and forbidding landscape of craters, mountains, and seas, void of any color or signs of life. At its crisp edge the moon's white, sun-lit surface was in sharp contrast against the blackness of eternal space. The images were historic and breathtaking, if not exactly comforting. After all, it wasn't cheerful entertainment to be reminded of the vast emptiness of the universe.

Then it happened. Apollo 8 continued its orbit around the moon's backside until the camera picked up something in the distance. It was a colorful body peaking over the moon's horizon. An arc of blue and white, it grew in size until we saw that it was round, and then we knew what it was: it was our earth. It rose above the horizon just like when our sun or moon comes up. *Earthrise* was a word we had never used before. Our planet ascended in the sky looking like a frosted blue ornament, not completely round, not quite full, but with a shadow on one side. For the first time we were seeing our planet from space. And it looked wonderful. The seas and continents were partially hidden by swirls of clouds, in a portrait of life, our home in the universe.

But that wasn't the end of the evening's show. The crew didn't need to be reminded it was Christmas Eve, and earlier in the mission they had been told a celebration was in order.

"Do you have in anything mind?" they had asked.

The flight director on earth answered, "Just do something appropriate."

And they did. In advance they had prepared a reading.

"In the beginning," one of the astronauts started, "God created the heavens and the earth.."

They took turns reading from Genesis, the first ten verses. They ended with, "God called the dry land Earth, and the waters that were gathered together He called Seas."

A quarter million miles away, we watched and listened to these inspiring words, not realizing that we had become the largest audience to ever listen to human voices. Then we went outside and looked up at the sky.

What a Christmas Eve it was. After what we had just seen on TV, there couldn't have been a better choice of text to express how we felt. On the night we were celebrating God's gift of His only son, we thanked Him for his original gift as well, His gift of life. We stood in our yards and stared up at the moon and, even though we couldn't see the tiny dot of the spacecraft, we rejoiced as if we were on board with our heroes. For a few glorious minutes we forgot about the problems of the world and instead thought only about God's grace, and about how precious life is.

We know that not everyone shares our faith in God's creation and the gift of His son at the first Christmas. We live by a faith that is not accepted by atheists. So, it was no surprise that after Apollo 8 returned home a protest was filed against the crew's right to use the spacecraft as a pulpit and Genesis as a sermon. We get that. But we all must believe in something, and it would have been impossible for anyone to have such a unique and profound experience as viewing Earth from a distant platform in space and not feel a deep emotion about the wonderful gift of life. The three Christians of Apollo 8 used Genesis to express their emotions. If they had been poets, they might have found their own words. But to them, Genesis was poetry.

After Earthrise, Apollo 8 orbited the moon ten times. It was now Christmas Day. On the last orbit, the ship captain, Jim Lovell, had to perform a precise rocket burn to escape the gravity of the moon and steer the spacecraft back to earth. The burn was critical. Failure would leave Apollo 8 and its crew in a lunar orbit forever. And because the task took place on the moon's backside where communication was lost temporarily, for several suspenseful minutes we didn't know if it had worked. The world held its breath.

Finally, Jim's voice was heard. This time, he secularized his message.

"Tell everyone there is a Santa Claus," he said. "And we're coming home."

Printed in the United States
By Bookmasters